T0288149

BRIDGING CAPITAL

FOR IT

ACTIONABLE WAYS TO BRIDGE CAPITAL INTO OUR UNDERCAPITALIZED COMMUNITIES

JEFFREY D. POWELL

jeffreydpowell.com

TABLE OF CONTENTS

ACKNOWLEDGMENTS

I thank all the extraordinary people who helped me complete this book. But, first and foremost, I am grateful to the numerous people within the public sector, private sector, and philanthropic sector who enthusiastically engaged in open dialogue over the years, thereby allowing me to deeply understand how the collective sum is greater than the individual parts. I am sure if I listed names, I would unintentionally miss one or two names, so I will refrain from doing so and give a big *THANK YOU to ALL!*

This book is dedicated to all of you who, in your commitment to balancing the imbalance in communities, have asked the questions this book has answered. To my wife, for standing by my side, supporting me to tell my story and the story of so many others, and to my children, who are strong, confident, and all a father could ever ask for—thank you!

Finally, but never last, I thank God for his grace and mercy throughout the process. Full disclaimer: I put the pen down multiple times in defeat or distraction while writing this book.

However, every time, God's still small voice would urge me to push forward, helping me to turn this manuscript into my book, a tool that will encourage and empower readers to take action.

I believe that if you are not a part of the solution, you lose the right
to complain about the issues. This is a two-step process:
read the book, then put the knowledge into action. – J. Powell

INTRODUCTION

"Bridging Capital for Impact" is a call to action for the balancing of communities—a deployable strategy that facilitates the collaborative power of public, private, and philanthropic entities, along with the people themselves.

Many have brainstormed ways to bridge capital into undercapitalized communities, though just a few have been able to do so. Having personally grown up in a blighted urban setting, where impact investing could have made all the difference, I want to help pave the way to a brighter future.

To truly be a subject-matter expert in understanding the flow of capital into undercapitalized communities, it helps when one has experienced both ends of the spectrum—economic disparity and financial parity.

In the context of an overwhelming number of global crises in the rest of the world, it is easy to overlook the impoverishment happening right in our backyard. I should know. I am an inner-city product of a disenfranchised urban community. As a youth, I watched our infrastructure crumble while other communities grew and thrived.

I wondered why.

Even as a youth, I knew that ability was inherent in all of us. I also realized that where opportunity is lacking, that ability is thwarted, and a great divide develops. Thus, the dilemma of communities that "have" and "have not" is a concern that many have attempted to solve. While a solution exists, it was unavailable to several generations of my family and neighbors trapped in this environment. Access to capital would have made a world of difference.

As one of the lucky few who transcended an undercapitalized community and went to college, I devoted myself to a career in finance. Specifically, to addressing the plight of underfunded communities throughout our nation. My goal as a scholar, financial professional, and African American was to become a creditable voice on this topic and speak from a prudent point of view.

My research indicates a way forward, a cohesive and applicable method to bridge capital to communities that need it the most. I devised a blueprint for bridging capital that can be applied methodically in any town or city while being customized within unique regional, political, and governmental realities.

The information within this book demonstrates a win/win paradigm. There should be no excuses with regard to raising capital for community improvement in our land of wealth.

No one should say, "It's not in the operating budget" or "Nothing we try solves the problem" because funds can be and should be accessed, and a plan should be in place. This book explains the plan.

Thought and action are each chapter's heart and soul and embrace a powerful concept I call the "ART of P4." It includes the following four sectors:

1. Public Sector
2. Private Sector
3. Philanthropic Sector
4. People of the Community

In the chapters ahead, I provide insight into each P4 sector, expressing how and why this is a collective rather than a singular effort. The scope is ambitious yet is purposely written in an easily digestible format. It is meant to evoke conversations around conference tables and discussions in classrooms. Still more importantly, my objective is to provide actionable ways to bridge capital for impact in the undercapitalized communities in the US.

Honestly, people are often the overlooked variables in an enormous financial equation. In this book, I share the inherent complexities and challenges when it comes to bridging capital. I also spell out the opportunities to do so and thus aid people in overcoming their plight. In doing so, we strengthen lives, communities, counties, and our country as a whole.

The City of Houston has provided many templates throughout the US to study and apply bridging capital. Some of the principles I use in this book are inspired by Houston-based initiatives but are not exclusive to Texas or the Southern region. They are applicable nationwide, including in my native New York.

This material, in essence, conceptualizes community and capital, offering critical characterization for each term. A community is defined by its membership and what the said members do to sustain and advance themselves forward. Capital is depicted by multiple examples that include financial capital, intellectual capital, human capital, economic capital, social capital, cultural capital, and environmental capital.

Financial and intellectual capital remains the primary focus throughout the book.

Perhaps the most helpful aspect of the book is that it is written from the perspective of someone who has walked both paths, one of financial disparity as well as that of prosperity. It is written from a pragmatic point of view because I have had personal experience of both.

I am telling you what I know, not what I think.

To conclude this introduction and begin the journey, this book is divided into five sections, which together chronologically discuss the past, analyze the present, and prepare the readers to take action to ensure a better future for themselves. Collectively, these chapters should be viewed as a roadmap through the lens of my personal exposure, professional experience, and overall banking expertise.

The book puts a human face to the numbers.

SECTION ONE

CHAPTER ONE:

The Need for Action, Not Talk

I have been on both sides of the tracks—the right side and the so-called wrong side, where poverty exists. When I was a kid, I did not realize we were poor because my mother always said that "poverty is a mindset," and poor was a word she simply did not use. There were times when we just did not have enough, but I never realized it because she ensured we had everything we needed.

I suppose most of the people who have not grown up on the "wrong side" of the track would see it as a blessing to end up in the suburbs; however, I believe that each side of the track has its value and that living both experiences has uniquely positioned me to be a creditable and relatable voice for change.

With this great calling comes a great responsibility to take action and speak out, so here I am. I emphasize that I have been on both sides of the tracks because I lived in the undercapitalized community I intend to help advance. This mission to infuse capital into undercapitalized communities is a heavy lift and will take resources, vigor, and consistent collective collaboration.

There is no question that we live in an era of remarkable wealth and opportunity, particularly in the United States. The flip side is that we often take our luxuries for granted. Many Americans can barely conceptualize daily life without the ease and convenience of smart devices, fuel-efficient cars, and electronic bill payment options. But what about those who exist without bare necessities such as decent housing, educational facilities, and food security?

The sad fact is that tens of millions of Americans live in appalling conditions due to a lack of investment in their communities, despite Americans giving more to charity than any other country per capita—$471 billion in 2020 (projected to increase to $510 billion in 2025). This statistic was researched and written by the Indiana University Lilly Family School of Philanthropy at IUPUI and published by Giving USA, a public service initiative of The Giving Institute.

Seventy percent of the money given to charity was through individuals, 16 percent through foundations, 9 percent through bequests, and 5 percent through corporations. The capital exists but is not allocated correctly to those who need it most.

This book is a call to action to bridge capital into undercapitalized communities with measurable impact.

As a youth, I did not realize the lack of infrastructure and everyday necessities most neighborhoods suffered from. Still, now that I look back, I can see that our local corner store made cigarettes and malt liquor readily available, not health and wellness selections like fruit and vegetables.

When we jumped on mattresses to play, we had no idea nor understanding that kids in the suburbs had state-of-the-art playgrounds. They had playgrounds in the communities they lived in that were funded by tax dollars from residents who resided within the city. Too often, growing up, we didn't know better. We had no understanding of how our expectations should be raised to enjoy the common good that was being enjoyed outside our community.

When we know better, we should do better. So today, as an adult, I deeply desire to help others understand not only the aforementioned disparity but how to bridge capital for impact into undercapitalized communities. My message is clear: facilitating the flow of capital into communities that lack access to funding is the process, and the outcome is a balanced and equitable community for all.

Impact Investing | Insight

It makes sense to begin this book with the principles of impact investing, defined as the active placement of capital in funds or companies specifically designed to generate a positive social outcome in addition to a financial return. Impact investments differ from funds that achieve positive social outcomes tangentially—the key difference is that impact investments are intentionally designed to do so.

The conscious application of impact investing is a relatively new concept in modern financing. During the 1980s and 1990s, the social and corporate responsibility movements built momentum that made impact investing viable and attractive to investors. Before that time, the goal of most companies and investors was to maximize financial returns. In the 1990s, investors in the UK made a practice of impact investing as we know it today and set an example. Around 2007, it was modeled by many investors in the United States.

The dynamic between the British and American models was initially different. It took longer to catch on here because the US government hesitated to assume the perceived risks involved in impact investing. It's rare to see the US playing catch up, but some would say it may have been good for the US to let the UK lead the charge so as to learn from their experiences.

Impact investing also gained steam around the turn of the century with the advent of microfinance as a developmental tool. The idea of investing in an undercapitalized community became a novel concept for companies and organizations that were focused on pure philanthropy. By linking social outcomes with financial backing from accredited and accountable investors, many undercapitalized communities experienced success far beyond that achieved by donors alone.

The recent economic crisis furthered the need for nontraditional investments. It called into question many established doctrines about traditional investments' risk and return profiles. Sustainability became increasingly important and inextricably linked to long-term financial success. Around the same time, government budgets dwindled, and philanthropists saw losses in the market. As a result, underserved communities could no longer rely solely on philanthropic support or public funding.

Fortunately, impact investors recognized the need to help others. Philanthropists saw the need to innovate. As a result, governments were relieved of the weight of total responsibility, and the resulting collaboration of public and private interests for the common good was a virtual win/win for all involved.

Generational dynamics have also played a significant role in *Bridging Capital for Impact*, particularly in recent decades. Experts point to a massive transfer of wealth to younger people, who, by virtue of their upbringing in a socially conscious culture, are open to investments that create social impact. To many younger investors, creating an impact in society is more important than generating personal wealth or gaining corporate profit.

Impact Investing | Challenges

With all that said, impact investing has been adversely affected by the recent credit market contractions. However, critical structural factors have enabled impact investing to weather the storm better than expected. Moreover, the same factors that spurred its emergence—the need for innovation, accountability, and transparency—have also ensured its favorable positioning for experiencing growth and generating even more significant returns when credit markets revive. Innovation, in particular, has the potential to catalyze mainstream investors and remains a vital component of the impact investing industry.

Nevertheless, the widespread adoption of impact investing as an asset class remains a challenge. The idea has caught on among a subset of savvy investors and funders in the US—particularly in low-income housing sector—but it is very much in evolution at this point and still not totally in vogue. Impact investing capital has some way to go before creating the requisite scale of a multi-trillion-dollar investment. According to Global Impact Investment Network, in 2021, impact investment reached $502 billion in global impact.

For decades, the industry has been marked by inefficiencies and distortions related to binary philanthropy or profit maximization. The legal, analytical, and financial tools available for impact investors and the language involved has tended to favor activity more reminiscent of the traditional model.

It is also important to keep investors' motivations in check. The notion of impact investing could quickly become a marketing tool for corporations and other parties wanting to raise funds to gain acclaim unless specific parameters and measurement standards are set in place. I firmly believe measurable results will inspire investors, enabling the sector to scale up over time. Whether or not achieving a grander scale will reduce the social impact or financial returns remains to be seen.

Tangible and Intangible Returns

Ultimately, investors' frustrations are also entrepreneurs' opportunities. I trust the popularity of impact investing will improve with education on the benefits of this powerful asset class—a double bottom-line return that will generate a measurable impact and marketable return for people and public as well as private interests.

The objective of impact investing is to attract substantial capital to generate two types of returns: (1) financial and (2) measurable impact. I call this the true ROI: Return on Impact.

The financial returns of impact investing can generate above-market returns over the long run. Beyond addressing meaningful social goals, the impact investing industry benefits the financial services industry by serving as an engine of social and economic improvement. Measurable impact includes the creation of positive outcomes like improving the quality of education, healthcare, or employment. It includes avoiding adverse outcomes such as spikes in crime or increases in illness and disease.

For individuals who live on the "wrong side" of the tracks, I pray this gives you hope. I have lived on both sides of the tracks, and my exposure and experience have led to my total persistence in achieving my aim of helping to streamline capital into undercapitalized communities.

My words should encourage and empower you, the reader, to make informed decisions on how to bridge capital—both your intellectual capital and financial capital that helps balance undercapitalized communities.

There is an emphasis on collective collaboration within this solution—we win as one!

What's the appropriate next step after reading the book? Take action!

Knowledge is power. The book should function as a tool to provide informative insight and call-to-action ideas for each of the P4 sectors: Public, Private, Philanthropic, and People (Community Members).

I intend to remain involved! However, you cannot get what is possible unless you commit to moving forward.

There is a pathway to revitalizing local economies and creating lasting stability in all communities. Encouraging actionable ideas on how to streamline capital into undercapitalized communities is the start. This must be followed by the execution of the knowledge and awareness retained from this book to help advance the efforts of balancing communities for all.

Why did I write this book?

The research indicates that there is a way forward, a cohesive and applicable model and method that can be applied in any county or city while being customizable to unique regional, political, and governmental realities. The model is called *Bridging Capital for Impact,* and I outline it here.

Generationally, it is time to rethink and evolve, reinvent, reinvest, and renew how we facilitate the flow of capital into undercapitalized communities.

Indeed, the pathway to revitalizing local economies has everything to do with creating lasting stability within our cities—cities with diverse "classes" of inhabitants. The upper class coexists with the middle and lower classes. The homeless are a class and a community unto themselves, and we coexist with them, too, perhaps uneasily or with a sense of fear and frustration. So, what are we to do with the most vulnerable among us? How can we bridge capital in meaningful ways that set in motion a trajectory of infrastructure improvement and opportunity?

I won't use the phrase "level the playing field" because I believe it's overused. Some communities just want a field, period.

The answers to these questions are the nexus of this book and involve key reference points that clarify actionable steps—the P4s. We must mobilize and prioritize capital allocation with measurable impact, and in the following chapters, I emphasize the "ART of P4."

We did not want a level playing field.
We just wanted a field to play.

CHAPTER TWO:

Bridging Capital for Impact – The "ART" of P4

We can educate others to empower them to make their own decisions about how they can make an economic impact. A community can change for the better with intentional focus and investment both in the people and the place they call home. A family should not have to move out of their community to find a community.

If a student in an impoverished community can go to college, return home, and invest in their community, their investment of resources into the community adds value. Their input on city councils; attention to the development of parks for kids, land, and zoning; and their investment of time and involvement in schools all add to the collective development of the community. We should encourage those who excel to return home and reinvest their time, talents, and treasures there.

When the tide rises, it should raise all boats—you cannot get to what is possible unless you commit to moving forward.

Collective collaboration has to come from each of the four sectors. If you don't engage the people, you can go from revitalization to gentrification. There is a thin line between revitalization and gentrification, and that thin line is the voice of the people who reside in the community. Most real estate developers' primary focus with community redevelopment is profitability. When it comes to choosing between their profit models and the people's primary needs, they will always choose the former. An example of this is the preference to building corner stores with a large freezer filled with beer and sodas vs. building a grocery store filled with fruits and vegetables.

It troubles me when those who become successful do not return to the neighborhood that helped shape them and mold their success.

I must preface this chapter with the Bridging Capital "Four" Impact model from which this book got its title. A commitment to the continuous measurement of impact, adaptation to changing conditions, and the capacity to stay focused long enough to transform the problem is a new approach and a powerful message. It is the platform for the Bridging Capital "Four" Impact model—the way forward for facilitating the flow of funds.

To clarify, when we speak of bridging capital, the assumption might be that we are referring to temporary funding that helps a homeowner repair their home from damage caused by a flood or a business owner cover costs until they can get permanent capital from equity investors or debt lenders. This has very little to do with the *Bridging Capital for Impact* model. Although any investment may have a temporary aspect, the model is not a short-term relief effort. It is more likely a long-term and sustainable process for a good reason.

Consider that some undercapitalized communities may take longer to recover and thrive based on, for instance, geography, culture, or politics. However, the strength of the *Bridging Capital for Impact* model is in its staying power, regardless of obstacles, until revitalization is achieved.

Community members and their community partners around the nation have sought, sometimes in a hit-or-miss manner, to derive funding and investments. But, no matter how heroic the efforts or how much "scale" one organization could achieve, it never would be enough.

The twenty-first-century approach to streamlining capital into undercapitalized communities can be transformed through the "*Bridging Capital for Impact*" model.

The ART of P4

While *Bridging Capital for Impact* is the message and the way forward for facilitating the flow of funds, the goal is collaboration between the P4s.

Just what are the P4s, and why do they matter? Well, we must mobilize and prioritize capital allocation for measurable impact—a blueprint pedagogy I call the "ART of P4." It has everything to do with actionable ideas on streamlining capital into underserved communities. The vision is that no person or sector has all the answers, but the collective sum is more significant than its individual parts.

I believe the impact wave starts with one ripple.

The one ripple is followed by multiple ripples, then comes the effect—the ripple effect — generated by the four sectors that comprise the P4s:

- Public Sector—the part of an economy that the government controls
- Private Sector—primarily businesses and corporations

- Philanthropic Sector—philanthropies, nonprofits, and foundations that exist to promote the well-being of humankind by solving social problems
- People of the Community—people in need, people who lead, "community quarterbacks," community partners, and community development officers

Together, the four sectors are the cornerstone upon which we bridge capital for impact and were first put in place in 2010 when I walked out of the doors of Merrill Lynch and into the doors of The Capital Maverick Group, LLC. They jointly reflect the knowledge and insight gained from professional exposure, life experience, and intelligence gathering to devise solutions for real change.

Collectively, we are more significant than the challenge! Therefore, in the coming chapters of this book, we will thoroughly dissect each sector.

The ART - Accountability Revitalization Transparency

Throughout this book, you will find many acronyms, some institutional and some derived from the P4 platform. For example, the "art" in the ART of P4 is an example of a handy acronym derived from *Accountability, Revitalization,* and *Transparency.*

- Accountability is taking ownership and eliminating the time and effort spent on distracting and unproductive activities
- Revitalization is the deliberate, organized, and conscious effort by members of society to construct a more satisfying community
- Transparency is the open and honest disclosure of information to all stakeholders; public, private, philanthropic, and the people

Since capital flows in the direction of least resistance, we must remove the obvious blocks and be prepared to face and remove the unknown blocks to distribute capital properly. We are tasked to produce results that can be measured and managed. We must identify and control risks early in the process to encourage the flow of funds (capital injections) into undercapitalized communities.

How?

The above objective will necessitate the deploying of solution-focused teams in cities across the nation to understand the many moving parts of capital distribution. These teams must know how to effectively merge the financial tools of banking, municipal bonds, government guarantees, foundations, endowments, economic development grants, private equity, venture capital, and foreign capital. Plus, they must possess guts, imagination, creativity, and leadership to solve the complexity of streamlining the flow of capital into undercapitalized communities.

This enormous pool of keywords and thought leadership is not as overwhelming as it may sound. The challenge is more significant than me and you individually, but not when we factor in the collective "us." Financial experts, economists, governmental entities and officials, heads of charities, community leaders, and the people—each of these will play a crucial role on the team.

We Win as One

Each chapter in this book seeks to identify the past, present, and future community economic development roles, the future role of each P4, and how we embrace and execute these roles.

On January 23, 2017, Simon Fraser University listed "The Five Principles of Community Economic Development," which is very much in sync with the *Bridging Capital for Impact* model and the ART of P4 collaboration agreement—sustainable, community-based, participatory, asset-based, and self-reliant.

The first principle is "sustainable." Community economic development, the *Bridging Capital for Impact* model, and the ART of the P4 collaboration involve analysis and planning to implement community resiliency through policies and practices for the long term.

The second principle is "community-based." Exploration of needs and community-wide planning focuses on individual participants and the common interests of the broader community—a "grassroots, bottom-up" process.

The third principle is "participatory." Our model and the P4 paradigm involve a broad, diverse group of members sourced directly from the impacted communities regarding "class, age, culture, gender, and ability." These many voices ensure all-active inclusion and participation as strategic planning and implementation occur.

The fourth principle is "asset-based." *Bridging Capital for Impact* means identifying all the community's resources and assets and bringing additional impact investments through the P4s. The funding available through the public, private, and philanthropic sectors and what the people can provide is crucial to implementing and meeting needs.

The fifth principle is "self-reliant." When communities begin to recover and thrive, the need for economic dependence lessons and an ongoing analysis of the flow of wealth "in, out, and within the community" will help identify how "leaks can be plugged" and "establish trade links" that benefit all partners. In addition, the investment provides opportunities to tap the abilities of men, women, and youth who now live and work in constantly improving environments.

People-Focused

As for the people themselves, let's not forget that "the same eyes behold different views," which is why we must seek input from those who live in undercapitalized communities. We need to understand what exists in their neighborhoods, study in their schools, shop in their stores, and then focus on solutions that incorporate their wants, needs, hopes, and dreams. It helps when one has walked in their shoes, bringing perspective to the reality of disparity that is detailed in the following chapter.

> *Don't let your temporary job*
> *become your full-time life.*

CHAPTER THREE:

The Least, Last, and Often Left Out

Many people are in need, which is why the P4s exist in the first place. Together we can make a difference, especially with the P4 approach to streamline the flow of capital into undercapitalized communities. People are the fourth P in the P4 paradigm, but I purposefully mention them first. After all, there would be no need for impact investing or bridging capital without human beings.

I've seen one deal change an entire community. A developer and shopping, beautification, and benefits bring in a diverse group of residents who are spending and active. For example, on Almeda Road in Houston, the area changed from a high crime community to one that features joggers, bicycles, people walking dogs, and empowered people today. The economic change encouraged new restaurants and high-end retailers, among others, to invest in the area as the entire face of the community shifted.

The People Perspective

But specifically, how do we identify who is in the P4 sector? I believe people can be concisely categorized as follows:

- Individuals who live and work in undercapitalized communities
- Those who run not-for-profit organizations, such as athletes, actors, business professors, and entrepreneurs
- Affluent members who return home and invest back into their community, exemplifying a "sweep around your porch" philosophy

Progress is made with courageous people who lead from where they stand and embark on a better path. The goal is not to gentrify or force communities to conform to outsider opinions but instead become better versions of what they already are by making use of the opportunities and choices finally available to them.

Those residing in scarcity need the brainpower and resources of the public, private, and nonprofit sectors to break the cycles of urban decay and underfunding. I cannot leave out the individuals who put their boots on the ground and work face-to-face with those in need.

We tend to lump various socio-economic factions together, resulting in raw data. What we lose in the process is the humanity of the people we are studying. I was part of that humanity and had no fundamental concept of poverty because it was all I knew. There was no other reference point, and I was a faceless number entrenched in an undercapitalized community.

A Firsthand Account

Looking back, my family and neighbors were "the least, last, and left-out," but I was blessed in character, drive, family, and love. Unfortunately, I was surrounded by limited educational outlets. We had one library that offered a limited supply of books and dim lighting. However, we had five basketball courts, three football fields, seven liquor stores, and multiple corner stores with bad meats, old milk and bread, no-name juice, soda, and all the junk food we could eat.

Oh, and let me not forget the overwhelming malt liquors and Joe Cool Camel and Newport cigarettes displayed and promoted as hip and cool. The wrong priorities were given precedence, and so generations experienced no other existence.

In my case, it was a mixed blessing to grow up in a community lacking the bare necessities others took for granted (i.e., grocery stores, well-funded schools and facilities, community centers, playgrounds, etc.). However, I was later placed in a position to know, without a doubt, how bridging capital into my community would have made a vast, almost miraculous, impact on my childhood. My mission ever since has been to do just that—route the flow of funding and investments into neighborhoods and municipalities where it is needed most.

Against these odds, I achieved a bachelor of science degree from the State University of New York Brockport. As the saying goes, you realize you're poor when you make rich friends—and in my case, I made friends in college who lived in communities with access to capital. That realization was a defining experience and the genesis of this book. When you invest a dollar into a community to install streetlights, you can expect crime to decrease. You can expect the talent pool to widen when you invest in a trade school that teaches students a specialized skill set. You can expect better overall health when you invest in a quality grocery store. The possibilities are endless. I wanted to be richer intellectually and monetarily so I could extend a hand-up and not just a hand-out.

By the time I graduated college, I had already begun to brainstorm ideas that would allow me to make a difference in the lives of others who lacked what we sometimes take for granted: access to capital. Thanks to a combination of hard work, good fortune, faith, and perseverance, I built a successful career in the investment banking field. I was so fascinated with the possibilities that I pursued and earned my certification in financial planning from the College for Financial Planning and secured multiple FINRA securities licenses. In 2022, I completed the Harvard Kennedy School Public Policy Advanced Learning Certification.

I was privileged to find the resources to break my family's poverty cycle, but I couldn't have done it alone. Others mentored me and served as an example of what can be achieved when we invest back into people. One person can make a difference, and collectively we can change the course of life for millions of people.

Disparity of Income

Although this book does not focus on poverty per se, I'd like to briefly mention the social ills of income disparity, as it stems partly from the exclusion of capital and unfair investment practices. Unfortunately, despite good intentions and many attempts over the years to "fix" the problem of income and investment disparity, the odds are still stacked against the poor. So, the real question is, *why does such glaring income inequality exist in the first place?*

An article titled *Addressing income volatility in the United States: flexible policy solutions for changing economic circumstances* by Bradley Hardy suggests that income volatility is part and parcel of the problem.

Published in the Washington Center for Equitable Growth, the article claims that "income volatility" or income instability arises from macroeconomic shifts alongside individual-level events such as job losses and gains. Low-wage workers and their families are the most heavily impacted and have limited credit market access and savings. In addition, low-income workers with children face a weakened cash-based safety net.

The author calls for reforms to the Temporary Assistance for Needy Families program (TANF) and the Supplemental Nutrition Assistance Program (SNAP) to enhance job training in sectors of high local labor demand, as well as the provision of financial and employment support, suspension of time limits on TANF assistance, setting of minimum state requirements for the provision of TANF cash assistance, and increases to SNAP generosity.

The article also recommends the following: (1) ambitious policy solutions for broader education and training as work-related activities within the Temporary Assistance for Needy Families program, (2) conditional TANF time limit suspensions, (3) an increase in TANF cash spending and responsiveness, (4) food stamp reforms, work requirements, and time costs.

From a financial view, I'm impressed that the author also suggests buffer policy solutions, including optional year-round Earned Income Tax Credit and expanded Unemployment Insurance coverage for part-time and less experienced workers.

Also published in the Washington Center for Equitable Growth on the same date is an article by Patrick Sharkey titled *Confronting neighborhood segregation*. The article states that in 1970, 15 percent of families in the United States lived in neighborhoods where most of their neighbors were either extremely rich or extremely poor. By 2012, the percentage of families in such neighborhoods had more than doubled. More than a third of families lived in neighborhoods considered chiefly affluent or primarily poor. As the level of economic inequality has risen over the past several decades, families of different economic classes have begun to move away from each other, literally, into separate communities.

According to the article, this "stratification" of neighborhoods calls for investment where poverty is concentrated, and *direct investments have never occurred* (emphasis mine). This is where my ears perked up, for investments in community infrastructure and the people themselves are one of the pillars of the P4s.

The article notes that the most consistent and expensive housing investments are programs such as the home mortgage interest deduction, "a tax subsidy that disproportionately goes to high-income homeowners in the nation's wealthiest communities." To confront economic segregation, he suggests minimizing its consequences by *shifting investments into every low-income community across the country* (emphasis mine). This, too, is a P4 focus.

**Honor where you are with
your best effort.**

CHAPTER FOUR:

My Truth, My Testimony

We often default to the public sector, private corporations, and philanthropies when seeking monetary help in overcoming poverty and urban blight. However, we cannot overlook the power of passionate and gifted individuals on a mission. Some of these individuals work within public and private entities. Some have established relationships with banks, charities, faith-based organizations, media, and law enforcement.

The human compulsion to "do good" cannot be discounted. The bottom line is that when individuals believe they can make a difference, they do. They help revitalize communities or enrich the lives of people who desperately want to achieve something more significant than a subsistence lifestyle. Revitalization breeds opportunity, and opportunity breeds results.

There's a standard quote in the lexicon: "Be the change." I've witnessed firsthand the impact that one individual can have on the people and the communities they invest in. When you invest in others through words, time, and transfer of wisdom, you move from just talking about it to putting it into action. You are the change. By facilitating that change, you become the change you wish to see in the world.

I am a living, breathing testament to the vast difference one individual can make to someone's life. An important person took a chance on me, and I was positioned and prepared when the opportunity presented itself to me in April 1998.

I recall my last interview that summer with a respectable investment bank, which later collapsed under the pressure of the 2007 financial meltdown. While waiting in the lobby with two other candidates, the hiring manager walked into the room and called for Jeffrey Powell. I stood up, and the man quickly noticed that the Jeff he was looking for was the only black guy sitting in the lobby. He looked at me, paused, and then said, "This should be quick." He was right. The interview lasted thirteen minutes, and he told me my services were not needed.

As I left the interview, discouraged but not defeated, I walked to the bus stop with my head high. While I was waiting on the bus to return to college, a guy walked up and waited beside me. He was well dressed in a dark blue suit, white shirt, burgundy suspenders, and a dark burgundy briefcase. As I admired his Wall Street uniform, I said, "When I get older, I want to be just like you." The guy gazed at me but never said a word. Shortly after my comments, a black Lincoln town car pulled up, and the driver opened the back passenger door for the gentleman.

I remember looking into the car and seeing two bottles of Fiji water and the Wall Street Journal positioned inside the middle console. This was back when bottled water first hit the market, so it was uncommon to see this combination. The gentleman got in the car, and right before it pulled away, the car's window lowered, and he said, "Son, two things: One, do not get old. And two, be better than me. I am not sure why you are downtown today, but call me if things do not work out. Here is my card." I grabbed the card without hesitation, and the car pulled off.

I call this a "God wink."

It was an interaction that would forever change my life in ways I couldn't comprehend at the time.

Two days later, I was sitting in his office wearing my favorite and only interview attire. This day the knot on my tie was a little smaller, more like the size of a dime. I'd never learned how to tie my tie, so I would slip the tie on and off my neck without untying it. When I walked into the office, he recognized my tie knot and kindly replied, "Son, who tied your tie?"

"It was me," I said, "but I haven't had much practice."

He asked me to untie it and told me we would practice knotting a Windsor Tie Knot. While going through the motions, his managing director noticed the act, leaned into the office, and said, "That is what you call leadership training."

He replied, "Did we ever hire our summer talent?"

"No," the employee replied, "why do you ask?"

"I think Jeff would be a good candidate," he said.

The manager smiled. "Good candidate or great hire?"

He paused, looked me directly in my eyes, and said, "I think Jeff will be a great hire."

"Call HR and tell them we've found our talent," the manager said, and that was how I entered Wall Street.

My new mentor, who later became a friend, had only one request of me: *Pay it forward!*

He left me his client book when he retired, simply because he trusted and believed in me. His philosophy was that you do business with people you believe, like, and trust, which was confirmed in this case. All these years later, I am still building my legacy, climbing, and taking action. Yet I'll never forget the power of that one moment standing at the bus stop and how one chance meeting can change the course of your life forever.

The trajectory from where I was to who I became was accelerated with the introduction of a spark. This spark in my life created a fire within me, and I rose to the challenge. I worked hard, invested in myself and my future, and built a life and family.

I have read many books, articles, and white papers on community development, impact investing, and general economics and noticed a common vein: many of the authors had never directly experienced living in an undercapitalized community.

To be a subject-matter expert, I believe total immersion in that environment is crucial to understanding the complexity of depressed urban living. I believe one must know it intimately to address it.

So, opportunity knocked, and I answered—an example of what can be achieved with the proper tools, training, and personal mentors who invest their time and treasure. From my early and later experiences in finance, I believe that when you align intellect and capital for the benefit of community revitalization, you are treating the cause, not the symptoms.

As a seasoned banking professional, I firmly believe the solution(s) for community economic improvement won't be solved with any one impact strategy. They cannot be solved with rifle shot tools like micro-lending, government subsidies, or social enterprise financing from financial institutions. In my opinion, impact investing is an asset class that deserves the same merits as any other alternative investment solution. It can unlock private and public capital and generates value in financial return and social benefit.

I have written this book to share my knowledge and insight and encourage like-minded individuals to embrace the "tool" of impact investing and commit to acting. The people who live below the federal poverty line are not just numbers. They are the inspiration and the genesis for impact investing. When we look into the eyes of our fellow human beings and see despair and hopelessness, it should provide ample motivation to bridge capital into undercapitalized communities. This book aims to help the reader better understand the ART of P4 and how it can help revitalize—and not just gentrify—a community. When you bridge capital into undercapitalized communities, everyone wins.

People do what they see, hear, and believe.

SECTION TWO

CHAPTER FIVE:
The Role of the Public Sector

Is it the government's responsibility to intervene in communities, or is it our individual obligation as citizens? The answer is not so simple. I have learned much about the importance of bridging capital along my journey and benefited from a vast depth of experiences. The places I've held positions in include some of the finest financial institutions in the world, from JP Morgan Chase in the executive leadership program to Merrill Lynch to Wells Fargo, where I am currently employed at the time this book was published.

This path has afforded me insight into the structure, inner workings, and flow of capital in corporations and communities and an intensive view of how global asset management versus capital markets works.

Capital markets are where individuals and firms borrow funds using shares, bonds, debentures, and various debt instruments. For community development, the most common capital is bank debt. However, their funding solutions must evolve as banks continue to expand to meet the ever-increasing housing, business, and facility demands of diverse communities. At the same time, the traditional sources of community development capital, such as government and foundation funding, are diminishing, and many community development lenders are looking for new strategies and techniques to raise money.

Some have turned their attention to accessing funds through nonconventional capital markets. Can this be done? How? Is it a good idea? In later chapters, I will address a few of these questions.

We are all familiar with the era of the Great Depression and President Franklin D. Roosevelt's New Deal, one of the nation's first examples of a government intervening in an economic disaster while at the same time aiding in public works and community development.

By the time President John F. Kennedy was in office, the Job Corps was in full force, allowing the youth to spend half their time in improving national parks, forests, and federal land and devote the other half to their education. Then, in 1964, President Lyndon Johnson's State of the Union address mentioned the war on poverty, which led to Head Start in 1965, which was carried on by President Richard Nixon.

Some forty-plus years ago, in 1977, the board of governors for the Federal Reserve enacted the Community Reinvestment Act (CRA). This act requires the Federal Reserve and other federal banking regulators to encourage financial institutions to help meet the credit needs of low- and moderate-income (LMI) neighborhoods.

Three federal banking regulators oversee the CRA and affiliated banks: (1) the Federal Deposit Insurance Corporation (FDIC), (2) the Federal Reserve Board (FRB), and (3) the Office of the Comptroller of the Currency (OCC). With decades-old requirements in place, the assumption is that the CRA should have greatly benefitted LMI communities. However, the nation experienced a shift against "public welfare" in the 1980s, perhaps resulting in President Bill Clinton signing the Personal Responsibility and Work Opportunity Act in 1996 to "end welfare as we know it." Aid to Families with Dependent Children (AFDC) was replaced with Temporary Assistance for Needy Families (TANF)—the same TANF program mentioned in Chapter Three.

This begs the question: what is the condition of LMIs today?

We find the answer by studying the Federal Financial Institutions Examination Council (FFIEC)—the formal interagency body that prescribes uniform principles, standards, and reports forms for the federal examination of financial institutions. In 2019, the FFIEC posted a comprehensive "List of Distressed or Underserved Nonmetropolitan Middle-Income Geographies" in all fifty states, American Samoa, Guam, Northern Mariana Islands, Puerto Rico, and the Virgin Islands. These counties and US Territories categorize poverty, unemployment, population loss, remote/rural, and distressed/underserved communities.

You cannot travel within
and stand still.

CHAPTER SIX:
The Public Sector Roadmap

Championing the American Cities Initiative shared in Chapter Nine, cities across the US have initiated their strategies based on the Blomberg Philanthropies approach. And while greater emphasis is detailed in *Section Three–The Private Sector*, the intersection of the CDFIs and the public sector makes the perfect spot to discuss the backbone of the first of the P4s (Public Sector) while emphasizing that every new endeavor demands that someone just like you take interest and help direct energy to a cause for a change!

Making a change for the better is a transformative endeavor, a life changer for you and the individuals you touch in your efforts. Martin Luther King, Jr. said, *"Our lives begin to end the day we become silent about things that matter."* So, speak up, be heard, and make change happen!

Not everyone will approach the transformation of a community in the same way. Some community development officers work with local governments to identify needs, from housing to water, energy efficiency, and housing redevelopment. They typically work with city planners after gaining community input.

Community organizers may spend more time with neighbors, defining common issues, including social struggles—especially those related to housing, infrastructure, and jobs—to infuse locals with the power to organize for collective collaboration goals.

Whether you plan to work individually or with others to inform your council members about the needs of their citizens, your roadmap to success must involve a result that benefits everyone. The first step may have been convincing yourself to get involved at any grassroots level, but the next step is defining your needs—and those of the community.

If you want your waste management workers to be quieter, call your councilperson. If you want to find a way to build more affordable housing, you must have more significant input from the community. Your needs assessment might involve the following:

- Affordable Housing
- Daycare
- Charter Schools
- Grocery Stores
- Medical Clinics
- Public Transit
- Public Safety
- After-School Programs

Or, your assessments gathered through casual conversations, public gatherings, school board meetings, and investment conferences may point to additional issues of unmet local needs you haven't considered. Regardless, you'll need to speak respectfully and intelligently about your concerns while also speaking from the heart to convince others about your concerns and commitment to fixing them.

Consider and convey what the community looks like in your conversations and what it can be transformed into with a bit of focus. What happens if changes are not made? Being proactive is usually much less expensive and more successful than being reactive. I encourage you to get to the issues before they become disasters, and keep in mind the local officials' perspective when presenting them.

As mentioned above, everyone will approach the steps necessary to implement change differently, but concentrate initially on the goals, not the minutia of each step. There'll be plenty of time to hammer out the details later.

Mission Statement and Plan of Action

By the time you've reached this point, you'll have specific goals in mind about impact investing and the powerful ways it can catalyze change. Of course, it is always good to have something in writing to tie those thoughts to action. So, what's first and foremost in your mind?

A mission statement defines your ideas by presenting what you wish to accomplish and the primary purpose of your efforts. You do not need to be wordy or overly detailed, but writing a clear mission statement will help you focus your thoughts on later actions. If you already have team members working with you, get their input. Remember, this will be a continuing statement presented to new members, volunteers, and possible investors.

With just a few well-chosen words and sentences, you can convey your thoughts and inspire your team, if you have one. But then, you'll want to think about how to transition from the drawing board to the goals you've set.

Aside from the ideas presented here in the P4s, the exact steps you'll take as a team should be represented as you prepare to assess and meet the needs of your community. Some steps may wait until you've got a firm grip on what is needed.

Your action plan could detail both informal and formal meetings with your team, finding a meeting space, establishing a business entity, preparing a website, connecting to social media, anticipating costs and future financial scope, and meeting with local officials and politicians. It's a process, but having some plans detailed in advance will help.

To expand and help you spread the word, you'll need to align yourself with those community quarterbacks who bring success—the champions. Every person on your list can help, but finding champions entrusted with decision-making authority in planning, financial, organizational, and media positions is imperative. Leaders inspire leaders! Never underestimate the power of the local big fish in a small pond to either champion or block your ideas.

As you fill those spots, spend plenty of time reexamining those early goals and exploring each new confidant's abilities and limitations. It takes time to bring people together, and it takes time to understand their motivations. Make sure everyone is on the same page, even if not necessarily the same paragraph!

Using whatever means are necessary, you'll want to consider roping in influential outsiders with excellent track records of communication and support. These champions may include community leaders, government officials, and like-minded and outspoken key public sector employees like fire chiefs, police chiefs, building planners, and local politicians. Those with time and passion can be great fits, while those with less time can be leveraged (it's not a bad thing) for their excellence with spartan photo ops or statements about the good you are seeking.

Most public figures are happy to throw their weight at community needs, primarily if they exist in the realms of public safety and housing, or even systemic inequities that have led to wealth disparities through prior planning that went amiss. Will there be hiccups along the way as individuals debate, potentially disagree on what matters most, and voice their opinions? Absolutely.

Remember, this is a marathon and not a sprint!

There's also a great benefit to gaining practical knowledge from existing (and successful) organizations or CDFI fund recipients. It's much better to learn from their mistakes and emulate their successful planning and implementation of those plans.

Do not try to reinvent the wheel—add additional spokes to the existing wheel, and it will ride smoother.

Find an Anchor Investor

While most shopping blocks are composed of multiple retail outlets, there is often an anchor store that can make or break a new strip mall. Often, the anchor is a grocery store. So, if your commitment to new development involves a grocery store desert, you know how necessary it is to have safe, local groceries for your community.

Not only does an anchor investor signal commitment to your goals, but it signifies trust and value to your entire project. Trusted partners encourage more interest and investment and pave the way for new research and conclusions about your community's needs and future.

Another great benefit of an anchor is stability. Your anchor investor has already weathered plenty of storms in the past. They've got data to share about expansion and investment and can answer questions your group may not even consider necessary at such an early stage.

Regardless of how prepared new community development groups think they are, there's rarely a case where more information is bad. Time may be of the essence in your quest to improve a community, but proper planning ensures success. Therefore, getting plenty of input on all the areas your plans may impact is necessary.

Continual Planning Benefits

- Gathering multiple sources of information on your project
- Identifying current impact investing in your geographic area
- Testing hypotheses successfully
- Exposing misperceptions about cost and impact
- Identifying strategic direction
- Reducing duplication of efforts
- Inspiring colleagues and the community
- Generating community support
- Attracting investors
- Prioritizing step-by-step goals
- Allocating resources
- Generating buzz and mass media interaction
- Finding new partners
- Identifying systemic inequities
- Establishing expected impact

Measuring Community Needs

Significantly few communities would not benefit from a comprehensive assessment of current needs. However, the approaches used to qualify and quantify those needs are likely to be skewed toward the assessor's background and upbringing. In layman's terms, "You do not know what you do not know." If your neighborhood never had a children's playground, a teen center, or a decent grocery store, you may not know you are missing out. Extending the needs assessment across a wide swath of the community is necessary to get accurate results.

To get those accurate results, community organizers and quarterbacks need to disassociate themselves slightly from their goals to see the community as a whole and not from the prism of their desires. There are several ways to manage those plans, including the interaction and interviews with community members mentioned above. Suggested methods include these:

- Interview community members
- Compare and contrast the community to cities with similar size and economic viability
- Employ spatial analysis (statistics) to understand geographic information systems
- Contrast overused services to underrepresented options
- Anticipate and extrapolate future demand
- Measure what's working to reduce duplication

These methods of assessing a community's needs aren't exclusive; there are other ways to find needs, but this list provides a starting point.

In other words, if there is substantial crowding in elementary schools, that's a problem that needs to be addressed, and changes need to be made to accommodate the factors of continued use and population growth. By contrast, fire services may not need to be expanded in specific areas due to reduced community growth. Some cities experience sudden expansion when a company moves in, and planning and infrastructure need to change to accommodate it. Other neighborhoods need essential services to thrive.

Interviews and Surveys

Although you may have made great strides in gathering community thought through meetings that can provide details and in-depth discussion, a more formal method of conducting surveys may be in order. Surveys can gloss over some ideas but provide the specificity and numbers necessary to make intimate investment and growth decisions when presented thoughtfully.

Any expansion of services or community development risks missing a critical need or providing something with a weaker-than-expected demand. Surveys can pinpoint what community members want and need with numbers and percentages.

Compare and Contrast

It's easy to compare a small city to a large one and see the disparity in offerings, but what about comparing communities of similar size and economic opportunities? When these are contrasted relatively and accurately, it can easily be seen what an underserved community might be in dire need of.

Then, based on community input, finding the critical needs that can be supported becomes easier. If there are specific services or retail opportunities in other similar size cities, you'll have the chance to examine why that community has enhanced economic viability. Be detail-oriented in your comparisons to avoid misinterpreting the data.

Geographic Spatial Analysis

Spatial analysis can provide a wealth of information about services and their geographic proximity to homes and residents. For example, a community with a single community center may have grown disproportionately in one direction, resulting in the center being a short walk away for some residents but a car ride away for others, thus reducing the number of visits to the center by the residents living too far away.

The distance to given services is a critical factor in community needs, but knowing a community's age groups and population centers will also enhance any spatial analysis and allow your team to see the overlapping services. Current US Census data can be employed to graph high-population areas underrepresented with financial or community services.

Overused or Underrepresented Options

A neighborhood with a corner market may offer some retail food products but comparing it to a full-size national grocery store would be erroneous. Not only are the product choices limited in the former, but the prices of the same are also never in alignment with those in the larger chains. Simply put, having only one choice when buying products in a neighborhood presents a monopoly and an inferior alternative.

Underrepresented options also include financial institutions. Many underserved communities have a plethora of fast-food options but no bank. A check cashing business is again an inferior alternative to a standard bank, whether the user possesses an inexpensive checking account or not. Paying high fees to cash a paycheck or using CashApp should never be the only option for exchanging money.

Again, the US Census can provide detailed data about the resident population, especially regarding affordable housing. Too many families in small apartments or single-room occupancy sites are a sure sign of overcrowding and underfunding. And the lack of a local bank can be a dissuading factor for families interested in purchasing a property or launching a business.

Future Population Demands

Understanding the future demands of a community is critical to obtaining the necessary goods and services for a quality life. Part of that understanding lies in extrapolating the population growth accurately.

Unfortunately, even the government sometimes misinterprets data and cannot accurately predict growth. Historical data is a critical predictive, but your plans to revitalize an undercapitalized urban or suburban area, expand public housing, or increase the number of services in an area can spur growth. So, make sure you include that incentivized growth in your estimations.

It's gratifying to pinpoint what's working in a neighborhood, and it's important to know that not every population center has the exact needs. However, when you see that the level of need is being met in certain areas, you are more likely to see shortfalls.

However, while your group can entertain plans to address those inadequacies, make sure those plans are based on the other criteria for assessing the community's needs. For instance, a small city in Nevada built a destination water resort because there were few water recreation facilities in the area.

Unfortunately, while addressing the need for recreation was a good plan, having a new facility that emphasized expensive "toys" such as

ATVs and quad riders, trucks with trailers, and boats was a mistake. The economic condition of the residents precluded them from buying large recreational equipment and thus doomed the entire project. The local tax dollars could have gone a long way toward constructing a city park and sports fields.

Financing Solutions

There always seems to be plenty of funding for upscale retail or service sector growth in high-income communities. Some reasons for this phenomenon are financial institutions, moneyed real estate players, and high governmental tax streams. However, the opposite reasons can lead to a lack of funding for an undercapitalized community.

No matter what steps your team has taken so far, there are a dozen avenues to consider for funding your project, and no reasonable, fair, and equitable solutions should be dismissed out of hand. One reason for this is the capital flow gaps that exist in many geographic locations. And those gaps (or capital limitations) exist for various reasons.

If your main goal is to provide more affordable housing, it's essential to know why there isn't enough to begin with. Is the lack of safe and affordable housing due to land shortage? Or is there a disconnect between local builders obtaining funding, hiring experienced workers, and getting the zoning changed?

Often large subdivisions will impact roads and traffic, schools and businesses, and fire and safety services. Unfortunately, even a single subdivision's tree, if you will, needs strong roots, good soil, and the ability to branch out. Those branches touch lives too—and require additional expansion.

Adding housing can bring people, workers, cash for existing businesses, and a reinvigorated tax base at the ground level. Those positive attributes of housing expansion (beyond providing shelter and lifestyle) can attract multiple investors, even beyond the public sector. Your organization may need to work with those investors, including social entrepreneurs, fund managers, professional advisors and consultants, education organizations, and even local public figures.

At the financial center, both public and private investors may include government public sector entities and CDFIs together with any collaborative groups you've identified. As a financing vehicle (mentioned at the start of Section Two), a City Budget as a funding source could include taxes. Payments collected from property taxes can provide multiple financing types, including value capture tools, tax increment financing (TIF), and parcel tax.

Value capture tools can provide long-term revenue streams to repay debt used for building infrastructure, such as transit projects. The Federal Transit Authority says,

"Revenue from value capture strategies can also be used to fund the operations and maintenance costs of transit systems."

"Value capture strategies are public financing tools that recover a share of the value transit creates. Examples of value capture strategies used for transit include tax increment financing, special assessments, and joint development."

Studies have found that transit projects increase nearby property values by 30 to 40 percent, and as much as 150 percent where conditions are ideal."

In the US, the public sector is responsible for building and maintaining infrastructure for urban development, including roads, parks, education, and public safety. When not managed efficiently, infrastructure frays from neglect and falls into disrepair. Although city planners get blamed for such disasters, the lack of capital funding, usually due to a distressed tax base, is a more likely culprit. As a result, underserviced communities are at significant risk even in the twenty-first century.

Value capture programs recover a portion of the benefits of public investments to offset the spiraling costs of the investment and proper upkeep and repair. The "capturing" is most often seen when new infrastructure investments are met with land and real estate increases, leading to higher tax revenues. Conversely, when tax revenues fall due to natural disasters, blighted areas, or crumbling infrastructure, whole communities are in danger.

As a reminder, Tax Increment Financing (TIF) is a value-capture tool used in forty-nine states (not Arizona). A city or geographic area can be financed to borrow money against anticipated future tax revenues driven by growth. The original taxes on the property before it is expanded or developed are paid to the city. In contrast, incremental new taxes help subsidize new development (including the extended loan debt).

TIF funding is most often used for growth items such as streets, sewers, streetlights, and electricity; land purchases; demolition; and clean-up. One of the chief ways of "selling" the idea of TIF funding is highlighting the fact that there are no up-front taxes for taxpayers to pay.

In Colorado, the Denver Urban Renewal Authority's redevelopment projects used TIFs to support blighted real property. Those properties skyrocketed from a value under $1.5 million to more than $5 million, resulting in more than $380,000 in property taxes from the pre-DURA renewal of $80,000. The renewal benefited the city, and the additional taxes benefited DURA and made expansion possible.

Property taxes, as those holding a mortgage or deed know, is municipal government tax based on the value of your property. Fairly simple.

A parcel tax is a special rate based on a parcel's characteristics. These are often flat fees, regardless of lot size or value.

In California, a Bay Area-wide parcel tax proposed to raise $500 million for San Francisco Bay restoration was rejoiced by some, disdained by others. Some felt the new twelve dollar per year tax would help deep-pocket Silicon Valley companies inordinately.

Although flat fees were designed to fund wetland restoration projects, flat fee opponents, such as Paul Premo of Mill Valley, said, "Equal charges per parcel fall unevenly and regressively on residential parcel holders because they would be assessed the same fee per parcel as deeper-pocket larger commercial and industrial parcel holders."

Measure what matters
"ROI - Return on Impact."

CHAPTER SEVEN:

The Shift – Money in Motion

The list of distressed or underserved nonmetropolitan middle-income geographies indicates we are a long, long way from eradicating disparity in our efforts to bridge capital. In addition, all states and territories have glaring, unresolved, and lingering problems with poverty, unemployment, population loss, remote/rural, and distressed/ underserved communities. So now we must ask, "What are banking institutions currently doing to encourage impact investment?"

High-impact community development investments such as community development funds (CDFs) and community investment funds (CIFs) are a convergence of public-private policies. For example, the Community Development Financial Institutions Fund (CDFI Fund) under the Department of Treasury was established by the Riegle Community Development and Regulatory Improvement Act of 1994. This bipartisan initiative promotes economic revitalization and community development through investment in and assistance to Community Development Financial Institutions (CDFIs).

Since its creation, the CDFI Fund has awarded over $2 billion to community development organizations and financial institutions. It has also awarded New Markets Tax Credits allocations, which will attract private-sector investments totaling $54 billion, including $1 billion of special allocation authority to be used for the recovery and redevelopment of the Gulf Opportunity Zone. Note that Opportunity Zones are a vital topic included in a future chapter.

Overall, through 2020, a total of $3.9 BILLION has been invested in disadvantaged communities in the US since 1994, with the CDFI Bond Guarantee Program backing $1.7 billion in bonds. There is no question that the money allocated is substantial, but communities must act together with foresight, vigilant planning, and oversight to keep programs running at peak efficiency.

Since the CDFI Fund's role is to expand economic opportunity for low-income and underserved people and communities, their investment supports the growth and capacity of a national network of community development lenders, investors, and financial service providers. CDFIs work to address these issues by investing federal resources that are matched with private funding—another convergence of public-private policies that promotes access to capital and local economic growth in the following ways:

- The Community Development Financial Institutions Program—program that directly invests in, supports, and trains CDFIs that provide loans, investments, financial services, and technical assistance to underserved populations and communities
- CDFI Bond Guarantee Program—program that issues bonds to support CDFIs that make investments for eligible community or economic development purposes
- Community Development Block Grant (CDBG)—initiated in 1974, a flexible program that provides communities with

resources to address a wide range of unique community development needs

- Bank Enterprise Award Program—program that provides an incentive to banks to invest in their communities and other CDFIs
- Native Initiatives— program that takes action to provide financial assistance, technical assistance, and training to native CDFIs and other native entities proposing to become or create Native CDFIs
- Community Facilities Loan Program—federal program that provides affordable funding to develop essential community facilities in rural areas
- New Markets Tax Credit Program—program that provides an allocation of tax credits to community development entities, which enable them to attract investment from the private sector and reinvest these amounts in low-income communities
- Capital Magnet Fund—fund that offers competitively awarded grants to finance affordable housing solutions for low-income people and low-income communities nationwide
- Community Development Bank, PA—bank that provides grant funding and liquidity financing for State Accredited Community Development Financial Institutions (CDFIs)
- Keystone Innovation Zone Program—an incentive program that provides tax credits to for-profit companies less than eight years old operating within specific targeted industries within the boundaries of a Keystone Innovation Zone (KIZ) in Pennsylvania
- Historic Preservation Tax Credits—a federal program that encourages private sector investment in the rehabilitation and re-use of historic buildings, creating jobs as one of

the nation's most successful and cost-effective community
revitalization programs

- The HOME Investment Partnerships Program (HOME)—the
largest federal block grant, designed exclusively to create
affordable housing for low-income households to states and
localities that communities use, often in partnership with
local nonprofit groups to fund a wide range of activities,
including building, buying, and rehabilitating affordable
housing for rent or homeownership or providing direct rental
assistance to low-income people
- Infrastructure Development Program, PA—program that
provides grant and low-interest loan financing for public and
private infrastructure improvements, transportation facilities,
airports, clearing and preparation of land and environmental
remediation, water and sewer systems, storm sewers, energy
facilities, parking facilities, bridges, waterways, and rail and
port facilities
- Neighborhood Assistance, MO—community or
neighborhood projects that strengthen economic
development and help fund job training initiatives and assist
with crime prevention, community service projects, and
revitalizing community-based buildings
and areas
- Michigan Community Revitalization Program—gap funding
determined by a needs analysis as a percentage of the MCRP
eligible investment basis

Microeconomic Planning

The P4s stress a cohesive working relationship between the Public,
Private, Philanthropic, and People who reside in the community
to be dynamically successful. We've started with the public sector

because financial investment is available from the US government through stimulus bills, and the CDFI Fund is the most substantial resource for communities.

In addition, the $1.2 trillion Infrastructure Investment and Jobs Act of 2021, signed into law by President Joe Biden, gives the green light for funding public projects across the country, from bringing high-speed Internet to areas that struggle with reliable broadband to fixing roads in those same places. In addition, $14 billion has been earmarked for low-income families to help them pay the cost of Internet connections.

Also, on tap are $110 billion for the nation's roads and bridges; $15 billion for EV buses, school buses, and EV charging stations; $25 billion for airport improvements; $55 billion for water supply improvements; $73 billion for power grid updates; and $39 billion for expanding public transit.

These investment numbers are staggering, and it is realistic to expect the projects funded by the Jobs Act to be implemented during 2022 and impact many communities positively. But, of course, that's a fancy way of saying that now is the time to look at your neighborhood and surrounding community and make plans to capture any available projects. As discussed in greater detail in the upcoming chapters, the people of the community significantly impact local projects and funding.

Moreover, since that funding and impact is at a community level, adopting a microeconomic view makes more sense than implementing the federal government's macroeconomic view. Microeconomics studies people's personal choices in response to incentives, prices, and resources. At the city level, the changes that come with infrastructure improvement impact current and future residents and current and future businesses.

There is a strong connection between new housing and traffic patterns, new businesses, local competition with existing private organizations, and public sector utilities like water and power, schools, libraries, public safety, and transportation. And what this means is that, again, a well-coordinated process to explore interest, funding, and development must be in place before implementing community support.

Much of that coordination starts with individuals, but city councilpersons, city planners, and politicians must collaborate to spearhead progress. Then, understanding (and planning) how economic development will change a community can be given even more precedence over the ideas for change themselves.

There's no sense in paving six new lanes of traffic to the downtown area and building dozens of new projects in the same sector if those new lanes bottleneck to just one lane a mile from their destination. Mom used to say, "Plan ahead; do not paint yourself into a corner."

When we know better, we do better. We can learn from the mistakes of overcrowded or poorly planned communities, and we can learn from successes.

This means that the process of planning must include collaboration from a variety of individuals, including those who have lived in the community and traveled those roads consistently. Traffic patterns, the economy, and how people live do play an essential part in economic revitalization. After all, in the end, it's not about the parks, trees, or buildings. It's about the people.

Collaboratives

How do we define impact investing? Does it differ in accordance with the market or community served?

The Urban Institute published a research report titled "Investing Together: Emerging Approaches in Collaborative Place-Based Impact Investing" by Shena R. Ashley and Joycelyn Ovalle and funded by the John D. and Catherine T. MacArthur Foundation. The crux of the report (a national field scan) has everything to do with impact investing and place-based philanthropy, with a general focus on underserved local geographies and states: "Through these collaborations, foundations are harnessing the resources and expertise of others who share their goals, creating new investment platforms to enhance the amount of capital that achieves both social and financial returns, and striving to catalyze systemic changes in the capital landscape in their communities."

Specifically, the report defines impact investing as "investments in companies, organizations, and funds with the explicit intention to generate social and environmental outcomes alongside financial returns." In addition, place-based impact investing is defined as "an investment approach centered on certain geographies that are often, but not exclusively, local." Finally, collaborative place-based impact investing "focuses on coordinating efforts and leveraging capital from across the community to enable different stakeholders to become part of a larger community-driven, purposefully-designed investment collaborative."

I was impressed by the following statement:

"Collaboration provides financial capital, intellectual capital, and human capital, but the real collaborative advantage emerges when inclusiveness and coordination are baked into the initiative to fill big capital gaps in communities. These collaborative initiatives can compensate for market failures, absorb risk for investors or mitigate risk for investees, and bring much-needed capital to underinvested communities where capital costs are often high. In addition, by creating diversified investment portfolios in communities, they can challenge the assumption that local investing carries greater risk and that diversification comes only from broad geographic scales."

There are a great many benefits to collaborative investing. While a viable portion of PBII success is achieved through each of the P4s, the public sector is a significant piece of the puzzle and a keystone of the foundation.

So, while the impetus of the collaboration and funding is to spur local investment, there is a general agreement that some investors anticipate positive financial returns. As the Office of Social Impact Investment in New South Wales states, "Where investors are involved, they will usually expect their investment to be repaid and, potentially, to earn a return. This return will likely depend on the level of social outcomes achieved."

The best part of their "practices" is that "Payments are normally made based on achieving agreed social outcomes rather than on inputs or activities." The true goal is obvious—improved living conditions for a community and the people within it.

Collaboration groups can begin with individuals discussing ideas and progress, networking with colleagues, forming groups to further their discussions, and including local politicians. They may include city and county council members and as we have already discussed, a business group or a community development corporation to expand the duties of those community quarterbacks can be formed.

A CDC is a qualified business, a not-for-profit organization that offers community services and programs that promote overall improvement. Community development is best based on the factors of human needs and rights, social justice, equality, and benefit for everyone. The collaboration of all people and their ideas is paramount to forming a working CDC, but planning is again a necessary core element.

Collaborative Benefits

The benefits of a collaborative approach to fixing and funding communities cannot be understated. Because collaborative efforts are a proven synergy between multiple people and groups, they are likely to have a much more significant impact based solely on their heightened scale of investment. But do not be discouraged; even small, well-organized groups can have a massive impact with strictly public sector funding.

At the same time, collaborative efforts are likely to include a broader range of ideas, backgrounds, and inherent strengths. By being more diversified, a homogeneous mindset is initially avoided as all voices are given a chance to be heard and informed on community matters. Developers may see the need for a new grocery store chain, for instance. Yet, the community member who has raised several generations in the neighborhood, owns the local grocer, and has kids now working in the local school system as teachers might disagree. While we cannot make everyone happy in growth and development, it's imperative to look at impact investing in a specific community from the inside out and outside in. All of this collaboration will be an authentic path to generating positive outcomes and providing a better life and environment for the existing residents of these communities.

In addition, any group, including investors, will display varying risk tolerance and income return expectations. As a result, such groups will likely demand expanded due diligence while sharing (and reducing) legal, capital, and organizational expenses. Ideally, a larger, better-organized collaborative group can attract more substantial investors and higher-quality fund managers and provide greater clarity on projects for all members.

We can implement our collaboration models on the basis of the collective place-based impact investing examples presented in the Urban Institute's report:

- Networks—exchanging information for mutual benefit; organizing an informal group of foundations to learn about place-based impact investing and its potential in the region
- Consortia—coordination involving formal or informal arrangements to collaborate on joint services to create efficiencies, enhance capacities, or reduce costs and begin altering activities for mutual benefit and to achieve a common purpose
- Alliances—more significant organizational commitments involving written and legal agreements, combining functions, and forming new nonprofit or private entities to reduce costs and give the partners more capacity to pursue an opportunity
- Platforms—types of alliances that benefit the collaborative group and connect accredited and nonaccredited community impact investors from the community to social ventures and funds

He that is everywhere is nowhere —
stay aligned, stay focus.

CHAPTER EIGHT:

Community – Cause for Collective Collaboration

Sure, we've advocated getting down and dirty to find what a community believes it needs. We've suggested that your friends and neighbors will likely have differing opinions, but when those bundled dreams come together in clear plans for the future, you'll have to garner support from the people you are trying to help.

When I was a child growing up, I lived in one of these underserved communities, and yet my friends and I certainly didn't see ourselves that way. Other kids may have had elaborate parks and playgrounds with wooden mazes or splash pads, but we didn't know these existed. So instead, we jumped on old mattresses and played on the streets or alleys. When I was in third grade, my teacher, Ms. Holder, asked me who I wanted to be when I grew up. She was the person who instilled confidence in me at a young age. "Great is who I want to be," I said!

Looking back, I can see that I probably answered with "great" because I had no real defined answer or role model regarding the man I wanted to become. And that's where the journey began. We did not have what other communities had, but we did not know any better. I did not see any barrier to becoming great. Years later, my grandmother would tell me to work hard, be accountable and responsible, and generate money the old fashioned way by earning it. This mindset was instilled in me at a young age.

Today, in many underserved communities, some Boys & Girls Clubs help fill in the gap.

Your approach to getting the word out, gathering support, and transitioning from ideas to plans to public sector financing may be a grassroots approach, and it's successful, good for you. It may be somewhat old school, but a successful transition from dreams to reality is all you are hoping for.

However, most industrial and community projects can be streamlined and presented in various ways that utilize social media. Facebook posts and groups might be a start. Connecting with LinkedIn is another option, as is using other media outlets like Twitter and Instagram. Regardless of which direction and how often you post ideas, present projects, or upload videos to platforms like YouTube, you'll want to stay true to your original ideas and brand your plans with similar messages.

Social media lasts forever. Keep repeating that to yourself before you post a single picture of a neighborhood you'd like to improve. Every post will be disseminated, critically eyed, and often misinterpreted. When that happens, who's to blame? Well, you are, of course.

That's because people will interpret anything you say or post through the lens of their life experiences. For example, if you post a picture of a tired, rundown neighborhood, some naysayers will complain that you are denigrating where they live—again because the idea of change is challenging. In the end, you've got to be able to post things clearly so that misunderstanding is reduced. And you've got to be able to explain what you mean slowly, clearly, and without insulting anyone.

You can do these things; it just takes practice. And it's one of the actionable ways to bridge capital for impact. A big part of branding your project and sidestepping the landmines of misunderstanding is being prepared to state your ideas expressly and honestly. A champion quarterback who can handle media (and you) when preparing ideas for discussion, planning speeches, and otherwise handling social media may be necessary sooner than later.

Then, as you get the words of your development ideas out into the more fantastic public realm, engage your audiences, ask for stories from audience members, and listen carefully for their words that can help make your case to financiers and government officials.

Your first event might be a handful of friends in your home or a local eatery. Or you can host a neighborhood block party. You've seen an issue, have ideas for a solution, and need to get people impacted by the problem to rally around you and your solutions. If you do not like public speaking (yes, surveys show that people rate public speaking higher on their list of fears than dying!), find someone passionate about your ideas to do the speech. Just make sure you are there to support them and then answer questions.

Your efforts in neighborhood speeches, canvassing, and social media should lead to interest from TV and radio stations. You can help get the ball rolling by courting any contacts at those levels, or perhaps you can begin with a local newspaper. Every station and news outlet has a community desk editor you can call or email. They need stories, and you need publicity. Get to it!

Working with Local Politicians

Mahatma Gandhi said, "Be the change you want to see in the world," and he lived that saying. You can too.

Most social movements and change start at the grassroots level: two people talking. Along the way, you stir up interest, get your points across, and look to social media and mass-market publishing to gather support. But, at some point, no matter how popular your ideas become, you'll need political support.

Politics is how goods, services, and privileges get allocated. The allocation rules may or may not be set at a local level, but local politicians possess some degree of discretion to choose how to allocate privileges and tax use. And it's often that tax base that can cement your development plans through TIF, bond, or CDFI use.

The larger your community, the larger the government bureaucracies are likely to be, but understanding the processes in place can keep you from feeling like you are banging your head against a brick wall.

Ideally, your local government is dominated by a politics of consensus, where progress means both economic interdependence and independence. Such a municipality may have already exercised its ability to listen to the masses, make changes where necessary, and set goals that trumpet the betterment of all citizens. Or such a place may only exist in the Land of Oz.

Realistically, the power of specific offices is relegated to ego and votes, and there are countless political hierarchies. Still, voters elect the mayor and the city council members in most mid to large cities. Then the council appoints the city clerk and the city attorney. Finally, the mayor appoints the police chief, fire chief, public works director, finance director, utilities director, and recreation director. So, your local political landscape may differ.

However, the emphasis of the mayor and city council is likely to be centered on finding the financing to keep things going as they are. If change is necessary, they'll get to it when they can. That's where you fit in—convincing them about the need for more substantial development in a timelier manner.

Extending public services like water supply, electricity, and sewer lines can be expensive. But doing so can attract builders and new industries, which attracts new residents to fill the jobs and broadens the tax bases of the city. Your efforts may involve providing more affordable housing, refurbishing existing homes, or capturing new businesses. Still, it's the local officials that will need to approve special tax inducements (or funding) for your plans. Fortunately, elected officials are there for a reason.

The primary function of our elected officials is to listen to the public and represent their interests. You're the public and have interests, so do not hesitate to contact community planners, the city council, borough officials, city representatives, mayors, and city planners. Your taxes pay their salaries so they can represent you.

If you do not know your local government, start by searching your city's website. You'll be able to see names, positions, office hours, and much more. If there isn't much on the site, call the first number you see and get information.

Attend the next town hall meeting and speak directly to your representative if possible. The meetings are designed for your representatives to mingle with their constituents, so the interaction should be conducive to striking up a dialog. Do not be surprised if the only answers you get are, "That's interesting," or "I'll look into that. " That's all right; you've got your foot in the door. If you can dream, you can prepare and gain support; you can gain traction in your goals to make transformational change in your community and your life!

You can start by writing letters, making phone calls, and arranging appointments to meet with local officials. If they are reluctant to see you or are "too busy, " go to their offices and camp in their waiting room. Be polite, be firm, and be ready to meet and greet them.

Without being arrogant, you'll still want to present your ideas to local politicians and get their feedback. Sometimes, an idea cannot work because another group is planning a similar effort, a tract of land has just been sold, or city tax officials cannot be swayed to incorporate your development or refurbish to suit your plans. Do not quit!

Cities answer to counties, so you can always take the next step in what may be a short or long process and move on to a county meeting. City councils usually have public forums and set meetings. Do not be afraid to broach your ideas (when you are ready) under one of those open-mike forums. You'll get the word out, get some instant feedback, and probably have others in attendance interested in joining your efforts.

Then, if that does not pan out, move on to the county meetings. A closed door or a closed mind shouldn't be the end of a good idea. Although getting involved in local politics may seem daunting, the people already elected may not know any more about the issues you want to impact than you do. They just got there before you did!

Improving communities and *Bridging Capital for Impact* is a big job. You've got to start with that idea, nurture it, make plans, get others involved, and roll with the flow as you will often navigate turbulent waters. And the *Bridging Capital for Impact* model is the preferred model.

Leveraging Public Dollars

There's always some reluctance by the public and the government to expend tax dollars for new projects, whether they are tied to local community investment, business capitalization, or infrastructure. It's the nature of the beast. There's never enough money to go around, and one mistake can bring disaster.

Over the past hundred years, the US has weathered severe economic storms. The Great Depression of the 1930s hung like a heavy yoke around the public neck for a decade until the manufacturing demands of World War II put seventeen million civilians to work in new jobs and industrial productivity nearly doubled. By 1944, the weekly take-home pay (including overtime) of people having manufacturing jobs was 50 percent higher than the same five years earlier.

Today we've got a two-pronged war: –one involving a severe lack of investment in underserved communities and one involving a lingering pandemic that refuses to diminish. The good news is that efforts to use the P4 model to bridge capital into undercapitalized communities through collective collaboration are a sound fiscal policy.

In 1989, David Aschauer compiled decades of data showing that the return rate of public capital was significantly higher than that of private capital. Moreover, the rate was much higher when public and private capital were combined.

When Bill Clinton made "putting people first" and a program of public investment part of his 1992 presidential campaign, he was successful in being elected and seeing the annual federal budget deficit fall each year.

Was Clinton's public investment initiatives the ticket to financial success? Some would say yes. Others would admit there are many moving parts to our government and finances, but the US economy and productivity did improve in the second half of the '90s. That is why we are so excited about your interest in *Bridging Capital for Impact*!

At the time of publishing, interest rates were at a historic low, and public investment is one of the most efficient fiscal supports for a depressed economy at local and national levels. Moreover, locally, investments offer long-term benefits for all community members. Those benefits can come from better roads (shorter commutes), water distribution, green investments, and education, all of which lead to higher productivity and a higher standard of living with hope.

Individually, your time and effort in embracing the P4s can bring about change that will enhance all our lives. While some changes— such as clean, safe drinking water and cleaner air—may be harder to measure in the short term, the long science will show healthier inhabitants and fewer medical issues over time.

Being Prepared

Preparing for your infrastructure project will take time and effort, but here are a few things to consider, especially if there is a mixture of public and private sector interest. First, no project is too small; everything matters, from planting trees and adding covered benches around bus stops to building a playground.

Firstly, keep your team apprised of what's happening. It's easy to run with the ball, but you'll need some blocking and an open field to reach the endzone. So, no matter your good intentions, it's better to be prepared and share your ideas to avoid mistakes.

- Plan for the long run—most projects take considerably longer than people expect. Look closely at your timeframe, especially with local politicians who support your project. What could change that?
- Community impact—consider all implications, both good and bad. Then, mitigate the negative impacts
- Job creation—will there be jobs created? Use existing data to demonstrate the emergence of new jobs
- Environmental impact—validate any possible environmental risks and find solutions
- Obtain permits—there will be a slew of necessary permits for most projects. Apply and follow up on all applications
- Return on investment—use a consistent, transparent methodology to estimate and track return on investment. These should include those tough nonfinancial benefits
- Federal guideline compliance—meet all federal regulations and guidelines, or risk losing public (and private) sector funding
- Demonstrate organization—public and private sector investors will demand assurance that their investment and your organization are sound procedurally and financially
- Monitoring performance—keep abreast of your project's progress from start to finish. Only an organized, structured business entity can ensure successful procurement of finances and continued investment and confidence with regular updates

While some of the above ideas may seem unwieldy, they are necessary parts of successfully implementing the P4s and investing capital in underserved communities. Many cities in the US have a successful track record of just such investment, all with exceptional planning and coordination at their heart.

Character is currency.

SECTION THREE

CHAPTER NINE

The Role of the Private Sector

The public, private, philanthropic, and people-focused "Art of the P4s" includes collective collaboration and each sector's inevitable (and excellent) overlap. We see this clearly in the foundations and nonprofits established by the banks themselves and in community initiatives that encourage impact investment through the following:

- Prioritizing Allocation of Credit (PACs)—community bonds used to increase the overall value with the ROI of property value increase and sales, similar to TIRZ's model
- CRA lending, investment, and service
- Home loans, SBL, CD lending
- CD and charitable giving
- Corporate foundations—grants, intellectual capital, and insight
- Micro-lending/loans
- CDC lending
- SBA loans

Defining the Private Sector

If the public sector of the art of P4 is defined as the part of the economy overseen by the government, the private sector is the flip side;

that part of our national economy is not controlled or owned by the government. Instead, it consists of individual businesspersons and companies ranging from sole proprietorships to multinational conglomerates that carry out their business across the globe.

Ideally, businesses are designed to create buyers, customers who benefit from spending their hard-earned dollars on a company's products and services. However, from a shareholder's point of view, the money earned and transferred to the bottom line is most important. Apple, McDonald's, and Google are hugely profitable examples of private sector companies that lay stress on profits and repeat customers.

Fortunately, some companies in the private sector—primarily when allied to community development and local economic growth—favor the human factor over profit. Which is a good thing because no matter how eloquently our forefathers may have warned us about the coming age (think Marvin Gaye's *Mercy Mercy Me – The Ecology*), we don't always weigh the risks nor hear the truth.

Tesla, while not as profitable as other companies like Amazon (although currently worth as much when measured by stock capitalization), may have far-reaching goals that impact customers as well as the economy and our ecology. We continue to hope the trade-off is for the public good.

Regardless of a business's ultimate goals, the private sector and private firms drive economic development through jobs, local investments, and gross domestic profit.

The Collaboration of Public and Private Sectors

The United States boasts the world's largest economy by nominal GDP and the world's largest stock exchanges (NYSE and Nasdaq—by capitalization and trade volume). In a country with vast natural resources and an economy driven by innovation and technology, that's something to be proud of.

Still, the country faces some nagging issues like crumbling infrastructure, the lack of investment in the inner city and underrepresented communities, and thirty-four million citizens living below the poverty line. Most would agree that the poverty line is set low enough to keep the numbers looking politically respectable while being atrocious and disheartening unless a single person in the US can live comfortably on $13,590 per year, the 2022 poverty level about $9,800 after normal state and local taxes in the contiguous forty-eight states.

Arguably, in addition to the about 10 percent of the population currently under the poverty line, there's another 10 percent that make slightly more but still struggle to make ends meet and enjoy a safe, satisfactory existence.

To combat the dysfunction often created and exhibited in low-income areas, a collaboration of the public and private sectors is necessary to create meaningful change for disenfranchised or marginalized communities.

The abovementioned combination of efforts is more than an investment of money and time; it is a lifeline for our future existence. Essentially, leadership initiatives matter. When we know better, we do better.

The Private Sector Insight

The private sector must work as a driving force toward economic growth, mainly because the public sector (government, if you will) simply can't finance every bit of the infrastructure our communities need. Why? Because the government exists on the taxes paid by businesses and citizens. If the private sector did not shoulder much of that burden or, more reasonably, that responsibility, citizens would pay for all government and infrastructure costs.

The US government's spending for the Financial Year 2021 was $4.829 trillion. If there were no private sector, US citizens would foot the entire bill, translating to a $30,757 tax bill for each of us. Fortunately, the US has a free market, a capitalist economy where the private sector thrives. And it provides employment opportunities to people who will spend their income in the communities they live in and pay taxes.

The Private Sector – Change Agent

The role essayed by the private sector has traditionally been a vehicle for goods and services. Fortunately, the private sector in the US is now responsible for much more than household goods.

- Employment: Private firms comprise 75 percent of the jobs in the US, while 14 percent of the total workers draw salaries from local, state, and federal government positions. An additional 10 percent of US wage-earners are self-employed, all of whom are a part of the private sector
- Development: Private firms develop industrial areas and are also the most significant part of the community infrastructure and construction. The infrastructure improves lives, provides employment, and provides a more extensive tax base
- Research and Development: Private firms innovate and develop complex technology that often takes years of research and trial-and-error to perfect

- Goods and Services: Along with essential goods and services, private firms provide the products we all use for health, comfort, and entertainment
- Education: While more and more private firms offer college-level educational services, many firms also offer tuition reimbursement and incentives for their employees to further their education
- Community Support: Private firms have a long history of providing monetary support to needy communities. With the Covid crisis, firms have recently donated life-saving instruments to the health industry, provided paid-for labor, and stepped up their commitment in various ways

Your Part – Collective Collaboration

There's no doubt that if you've navigated your way through this explanation and insight on the need for bridging capital to under-capitalized communities, you've got a goal of your own. That plan or dream likely goes well beyond what you've come to see in this book as a pathway to success. So, if it's encouragement that you need, we know you've got the grit and have resolved to reach the next step. You wouldn't be reading this if you didn't. And this book serves as the blueprint.

At the same time, our towns and cities need your help. Unfortunately, we cannot convince everyone about the moral imperative to make the necessary changes in our undercapitalized communities. However, with your drive, and determination, you are bound to succeed, and your success will communicate the very essence of our message to others near you and make the overall transformation a reality.

The overall collective collaboration between you (as the private sector) and the public sector (as well as the philanthropic and peo-ple-focused parts of the P4s) are what makes a dream come true. No man or woman is an island. It takes a community to raise a child, and it takes that same collaboration to revitalize a local economy into a healthy place we'd all like to live in. And it starts with you!

So, think about your goal and how it intersects with that thriving neighborhood in your mind's eye. We need safety; stability; economic growth; good jobs; transportation; education; affordable housing; parks; playgrounds; grocery stores whose goal is to feed, not gouge; local financial institutions; and community activities. Is this too much to ask for?

What about healthcare and our environment? Unfortunately, our government was not designed to fix our woes and transform society. That starts with us, even if all we want to accomplish this year is to plant a few shade trees to oxygenate our atmosphere and shade our bus stop benches. There's nothing wrong with starting small.

Fortunately, some businesses are practicing more cultural responsibility. They, too, started small and grew their ideas for social practices to include their impact on all of us.

**When God gives you an opportunity,
what you do with it is your gift to him.**

CHAPTER TEN:

TMI – Time, Money, and Impact

Corporate Social Responsibility or CSR is a private firm practice of social responsibility that can refer to local support, eco-friendliness, and other beneficial societal impacts. Social accountability favors businesses as customers place a premium on businesses implementing important CSR. Employees also take pride in working for companies that lower their carbon footprint, increase cultural awareness, and allow workers to balance family time with work efforts and provide good wages.

Being good corporate citizens benefits everyone and is an excellent step toward seeing change, especially in marginalized neighborhoods. Sometimes the difference between a good neighbor and a great neighbor is the people in the community who use the benefits of the P4s to enhance corporate awareness and drive successful collaboration between the P4 sectors.

According to CSR Communications, the 2020 CSR research, 79 percent of those polled expected businesses to continue to improve their CSR efforts, and nearly 70 percent said that those businesses "should take actions to improve issues that may not be relevant to everyday business operations."

In addition, 87 percent said they would buy a product if a company advocated for an issue they supported. In comparison, 76 percent said they would refuse to purchase a product if they found out a company supported an issue contrary to their beliefs.

Important corporate responsibility includes popular practices that resonate with employees, customers, and stakeholders.

- Environmental Footprint: Reducing a company's carbon footprint through reduced power needs, alternative fuels, reduced waste (packaging, loss, overproduction), efficient work schedules, and other efforts benefit the business and society
- Transparency: Involving employees at all levels in its decision-making processes and allowing consumers to see all aspects of CSR brings reliability and clarity to a business brand
- Philanthropy: Donations of supplies and services, as well as money, are an excellent social responsibility practice, but committing to local infrastructure projects is the golden ticket to heightened CSR awareness in a community
- Sustainability: Not every business can replicate or replace the raw materials it uses, but Boise Cascade Wood Products, LLC, is a good neighbor/supplier. The company practices standards outlined by the Sustainable Forestry Initiative® while contributing to the continuous improvement of science through research
- Prioritizing Social Justice: Domestic job growth is the highest action consumers ask of corporations, but rounding out the top four are racial equality, women's rights, and the cost of higher education

Small businesses without deep pockets can significantly impact a local community, primarily if they work together.

CSR can improve its branding, giving it a responsible, healthy image. Good neighbors are treated well, and good companies often see community support in sales numbers and social media attention. The employees working for a responsible company also command respect in their community, which in turn translates into high employee morale.

Recently, many biopharmaceutical companies such as Moderna and Pfizer have dominated newscasts and social media platforms for their efforts in combating Covid-19. Johnson & Johnson has also been at the forefront, but then it was already a champion of some environmentalists for investing in alternative energy sources to reduce environmental impact.

Likewise, Google calls itself carbon neutral after investing heavily in renewable energy sources and sustainable offices.

TOMS shoes employ a "one for one concept," where the company promises to deliver a free pair of shoes to a child in need for every sale they make.

Lego is investing millions of dollars in climate change studies and reducing waste. Toward that end, they now use bio-derived polyethylene to make their botanical elements and have ceased using single-use plastic bags.

Newman's Own, a food company founded by Paul Newman and A. E. Hotchner, donates 100 percent of its after-tax profits to the Newman's Own Foundation and supports educational and charitable organizations. To date, the company has donated over half a billion dollars to charities.

If your goal is to improve the environment on a global scale, aligning yourself with any socially responsible company can be beneficial.

Every company can positively impact a community, and every individual who follows *Bridging Capital for Impact* social responsibility motives is likely to be viewed more favorably. When you can dig down to the root cause of some issues, the community will back you in your improvement initiatives.

Now suppose there have been several fender benders in a section of your neighborhood, along with other residents who commit minor crimes like graffiti and vandalism. Is the problem the education system? Or is it a lack of jobs? Perhaps there are fewer jobs in the area because the retail area is blighted, the sidewalks are cracked, and the lighting is poor.

Can you and your councilperson petition for new streetlights? How about getting the sidewalks fixed? How about striping the parking spaces to reduce the scratched fenders? Maybe there can be a trade-off with the city paying for the improvements but installing parking meters. Will the retail sector now revitalize the block and put more people to work?

Maybe now you buy a storefront, open a business, or buy a building—even if it needs to be rebuilt. And how do you do that? By collaborating with the public sector and likely working with an impact investor.

Whether you are working with a city for tax increment financing (TIF) for streetlights, sidewalks, and street repairs, or private investors bringing in funds for building repairs, be adamant about realistic terms, goals, and income streams.

Remember, the ART of P4s comprises Accountability, Revitalization, and Transparency. You take accountability for streamlining your activities by eliminating unproductive actions and go straight to the revitalization of an area in need while staying transparent in your actions. You're the community quarterback. You've got to call the plays.

As outlined in Chapter Six Roadmap to the Public Sector, your job as a community organizer or local quarterback takes time and commitment. Still, there are distinct advantages to getting the ball rolling.

As for other ways of bridging capital to your project and community, the main idea of government CDFI funds is to revitalize distressed areas. And there are more than a thousand CDFIs nationally. Also available are the CDFI Bond Guarantee Program and the Community Development Block Grant (CDBG) program you can tap into.

In addition, several national and multinational banking institutions have begun programs to revitalize underrepresented places with aggressive loan and grant programs waiting to be accessed.

Compassion for a need brings
commitment to the vision.

CHAPTER ELEVEN:
Conscious Capital, Beyond The Checkbook

Complementing the banking communities' outreach efforts, investment banking funds are increasingly turning to social programs and offering socially sustainable financing or funds representing environmental, social, and governance (ESG) fronts.

Many investors steer at least some of their cash toward specific industries—real estate, tech, manufacturing—and more funds are grappling with renewable energy, remanufacturing, and recycling, leading to an even bigger dominance of ESG financing.

While ESG financing may not directly correlate to private sector bridging for communities, there is some confluence of ideas and the possibility that at the core of funding for specific programs and infrastructure, an ESG designated fund could be utilized. Regardless, the emergence of a socially responsible set of investment strategies that push (or at least champion) socially relevant and environmentally kind government (public sector) structures is welcome.

Relevant and successful ESG funds comprise companies that reduce their carbon footprint, are socially aligned, and follow policies that minimize any harmful environmental impact. However, fund managers sometimes support companies that can improve their ESG standing but show great efforts regarding heading in the right direction. Fund managers are also outspoken and can drive meaningful dialogue with businesses to improve their environmental impact.

ESG fund managers typically covet specific governmental commitments, including business ethics and transparency, high reporting history, and shareholder rights. The actual direction and composition of the board of directors are also considered. An experienced board is essential, but so is a rounded, diversified say in running the company.

For those of you considering holding a position in an ESG fund personally or in conjunction with any business that might be going forward with *Bridging Capital for Impact* in a community you want to serve, keep in mind that your portfolio will likely be scrutinized by a wide variety of citizens and business entities. Therefore, your alignment with the right side of history and business practices is critical.

Things to Consider:

- Some funds don't have ESG in their name but follow excellent environmental, social, and governance practices
- Most funds have some higher and lower-scoring ESG holdings
- A fund's performance may not mirror overall market conditions due to holdings
- Many environmentally stringent companies have a longer lag time as regards profitability
- Due diligence is mandatory as funds weigh each ESG category differently

- Always view an ESG fund's current holdings to verify your comfort level with their choices
- Verify expense ratios and how its ESG focus may affect its risk
- Verify how the fund weighs each E-S-G factor in portfolio holdings
- Keep in mind that different third-party companies and research groups "score" ESG funds but may also have their agenda

In addition, consider how an ESG fund and its company holdings treat its workers and customers, and of course, the community, environment, and shareholders.

SRI - Socially Responsible Investing

Socially responsible investing (SRI) helps investors choose stocks and funds that match their values. While ESG funds can be an excellent match, SRI is a more precisely guided approach to specific beliefs.

When CVS Pharmacy decided to remove tobacco products from their stores, Wall Street anticipated a possible drop in their profitability and a reduced share value. Instead, although tobacco sales were a significant part of CVS's profits, their sales plateaued instead of falling, and their share values rose, perhaps because some investors wanted to support the changes.

Specific ESG funds may or may not have given the tobacco sales specific weight for or against holding CVS but may have already invested in the parent CVS Health on the basis of corporate performance only.

Impact Investing

As the name suggests, impact investing is essentially impact-based investing. Investors choose market segments such as green energy, housing equity, and healthcare access, focusing on the life-improving aspects of these segments instead of only the investment returns accruing from them.

Ideally, any investment has a positive return, but knowing that the companies you support and invest in effect positive social and environmental changes is a plus. As mentioned earlier, these companies may be slower to show profits than less-consciously aligned companies or funds due to the specific environmental challenges they face.

Conscious Capitalism

Also, ideally, companies should act in the world's best interests, but it rarely happens. According to Oxfam International, 42 individuals held the same wealth as 3.7 billion people of the world's poorest in 2017. At the same time, 82 percent of the global wealth generated went to the wealthiest 1 percent of individuals.

In 2022 terms, the combined wealth of the world's top 10 billionaires doubled during the pandemic and is now six times greater than that of the world's poorest 3.1 billion people. Most rich individuals consider it fair capitalism. Those on the other side question the equity ethics of such staggering disparities in wealth.

Raj Sisodia, a marketing professor, and John Mackey, the co-founder of Whole Foods, first broached this subject and named the belief in conscious capitalism necessary ethics in pursuing profits.

They consider the four most important parts of conscious capitalism to be evident in the following:

- Higher purpose—"Elevating humanity through business begins with knowing WHY your company exists. Without this, you have no compass to find and stay focused on your True North. Businesses should exist for reasons beyond just making a profit. We see profit as a necessary means to achieving your purpose—not as an end in and of itself."

- Stakeholder orientation—"Recognizing the interdependent nature of life and the human foundations of business, a business needs to create value with and for its various stakeholders (customers, employees, vendors, investors, communities, etc.)."

- Conscious leadership—"Human social organizations are created and guided by leaders – people who see a path and inspire others to travel along the path. Conscious Leaders understand and embrace the Higher Purpose of business and focus on creating value for and harmonizing the interests of the business stakeholders. In addition, they recognize the integral role of culture and purposefully cultivate Conscious Culture."

- Conscious culture—"This is the ethos—the values, principles, practices—underlying the social fabric of a business, which permeates the atmosphere of a business and connects the stakeholders to the purpose, people, and processes that comprise the company. All companies have a culture, but not all companies intentionally develop a culture that promotes their values and purpose."

What Conscious Capitalism, Inc. has defined (or divined) is an ideal construct of business that many people can embrace, especially when working toward the greater good of those in underrepresented areas. Unlike the P4s, specific individuals will work tirelessly to correct wrongs, correct flaws, and improve the world—often starting with a tiny neighborhood at a time.

There is no nobler goal than freeing the oppressed, opening the doors of freedom, and making meaningful changes in others' lives. *Bridging Capital for Impact* holds all these ideals and can bring about real change that has been withheld for so long—for so many.

MDI Banks and the Great Recession

While it is encouraging to see large banks committed to investing in underserved communities, it's just as discouraging to see that Minority Depository Institutions (MDIs) often take the brunt of financial calamities. During the Great Recession (2008 to 2015), the number of MDIs fell from 219 banks to just 171. The highest percentage of closed MDIs was among African American-owned banks.

The need for local bank representation in all communities, especially those underserved by the financial sector, is critical to economic stability and growth. Without local lenders, how can businesses thrive? In addition, MDIs originate a greater share of small business loans in census tracts with a higher minority population than non-MDIs. And what to do when there are no banks?

From 2000 to 2015, while there was a fall in the number of banks nationwide, an astonishing 60 percent of banks with assets under $100 million disappeared. The business consensus is that MDIs with less than $100 million in assets perform worse than other banks. Of course, when compared to older, financially structured behemoths, almost any business would also fare worse. Banks are challenged in financially tight times to find their working capital, mainly when serving smaller investors. But there are other issues.

In 2009, when the Troubled Asset Relief Program (TARP) program was passed by Congress and signed into law by President George Bush, the idea was that the government would purchase toxic assets and equity from financial institutions to prop up the financial sector. Great idea, but not equitable performance!

Of the $475 billion authorized, $205 billion went toward purchasing bank equity shares Then $68 billion went toward purchasing shares of the American International Group (AIG), $45 billion to Citigroup and Bank of America, $80 billion (loans and capital injections) to automakers, $22 billion toward mortgage-related securities, and $46 billion toward homeowner foreclosure assistance.

If you wonder how much went to MDIs and small banks, it was virtually nothing. The $600 million in capital allocated under the Community Development Capital Initiative (CDCI) to banks that served disadvantaged communities was frighteningly small. It was 12 percent of the $475 billion in bailouts.

While some of the assets of MDIs were acquired through mergers or failures by other MDIs, most were not. And only one new MDI was started: the Urban Partnership Bank, headquartered in Chicago. In 2011 it was certified as a community development financial institution (CDFI).

Unfortunately, the banks that underwrite mortgages in marginalized cities are forced to release assets when the broader market downturns. This usually happens when mark-to-market accounting is used, which values assets at today's price. In the case of Chicago's Shore Bank, their asset ratio ballooned, causing insolvency when the bank was taken over, with investments from Bank of America, Citigroup, Goldman Sachs, JP Morgan Chase, and Morgan Stanley. Saviors? Not exactly.

The investments placed by those prominent banks saw significant return potential for well-financed national institutions. Instead, as often happens during economic turmoil, those most in need, often in underfunded neighborhoods, lose whatever equity they have while the seemingly wealthiest sectors of society come out smelling like roses as their investments during downtimes blossom into two- and three-fold increases as the economy recovers.

The story doesn't end there unless we allow it to. There is much to be done in our hometowns and municipalities, so be enthusiastic about ideas for refurbishing, building, or collaborating with the public and private sectors to start a new development project.

That rush of excitement you feel at the possibility of bringing about development is the first step on the pathway to revitalizing local economies and creating lasting stability in undercapitalized communities.

Infrastructure – Collaboration between Public and Private Sector

As discussed in Section Two, collaboration between the public and private sectors is necessary and creates a redefined and level playing field when implemented with social consciousness. President Biden's primary objective in his push to win the presidency (along with vanquishing Covid-19) was to implement comprehensive infrastructure studies followed by massive projects to replace and improve crumbling public sector projects, from roads and highways to airports and waterways.

The Build Back Better bills bandied about in Congress during late 2021 and early 2022 promised an initial funding of over $500 billion targeted toward improving our country's infrastructure.

Unfortunately, the bill was heavily weighted with other projects—green energy, literacy programs, free pre-K classes, $250 child tax credits, mandatory 6x-match political contributions—and hit roadblocks in the legislature.

However, the need for considerable investments in infrastructure and repairing urban decay are self-evident in the US and many nations across the globe. And the dollars necessary to improve essential services like power, water, and telecommunications are expected to top 3.8 percent of the GDP through 2030. Climate change issues are likely to dwarf that total capital committed.

According to McKinsey & Company, new demand for labor in infrastructure and buildings could soon create eighty million jobs worldwide, mostly in the fields of architecture and engineering, in the electrical and carpentry trades, and in other construction and skilled trade groups.

Whether that sounds like good news or not is subjective. But it does point to the fact that many areas need new infrastructure. More firms are gaining (excuse me) a social conscience and emphasizing economically and socially necessary projects instead of always emphasizing those that are economically viable and likely to pad the bottom line.

Fortunately, civic projects are often backed by the public sector, translating to successful CDFI investment. Remember, Community Development Financial Institutions (CDFIs) are private-sector financial institutions. They mainly focus on personal lending and business development in under-capitalized or marginalized communities and receive federal funding through the US Department of the Treasury.

The confluence of the two entities, private and public, into a cohesive unit to manage our nation's infrastructure seems simple when viewed from the outside, far away from drawing boards, congressional oversight, and financial planning groups. The highways get proposed and built, and we drive on them when they're available. But the overall history, structure, and successful implementation of each project stretched across our vast nation are mindboggling.

Not to bore you with history and details, but whether you are going to champion your cause, establish a community group to support neighborhood efforts, or create a business to manage financing, procurement, planning, or actual construction, there are some elements of government—and how they can intersect with the P4s—that are helpful to know in advance.

There aren't any specific words in the US Constitution that describe the infrastructure. Still, the Constitution does explain the rights and responsibilities of the state governments and their relationship to the federal government. Wrapped in that wording and each state's constitutions, statutes, and amendments is a working relationship that broadly defines the utilities (and structures and facilities) necessary for continued satisfactory public service.

Toward that end, the federal government first authorized, via Congress, the construction of the National Road in 1806. Sometimes it seems as though that road hasn't been repaired since it was built, but it was, after all, built entirely with federal money.

While federal money does come from fees and interest (plus duties and excise taxes), the largest source of revenue comes from taxes—income taxes paid by individuals, payroll taxes paid by employers and workers, and corporate taxes paid by businesses. Taxes are the federal government's largest source of income (or revenue). The government does receive income from other sources (like fees and interest), but those sources are dwarfed by what we all pay in taxes.

Payroll taxes become part of trust funds set aside for Social Security, Medicare, and the Highway Trust Fund derived from gasoline taxes. But it's never enough. The federal government spends much more than it ever brings from tax revenues and borrows to finance the rest. So, the treasury borrows money by issuing bonds.

The sale or transfer of treasury bonds helps the government cover federal costs and adds to the national debt.

As for infrastructure, the Bureau of Economic Analysis (BEA) defines three subsets of infrastructure figures for 2017 federal and state spending:

- Basic—42 percent or $326 billion for things like transportation, waterways, and utilities
- Social—32 percent or $246 billion for things like schools, libraries, and hospitals
- Digital—26 percent or $197 for things like the storage and exchange of data through a centralized communication

The federal government directly spends on the infrastructures it owns, such as traffic control systems, waterways, and dams. However, it also spends on grants and loans to state and local governments and allows them to issue tax-exempt loans.

More specifically, transportation spending comes from the same state and local governments. In 2020, the federal government spent $63 billion on transportation and granted $83 billion to state and local governments for transportation infrastructure funding. At the same time, private firms handled the bulk of the construction, providing jobs and an additional tax base from selling materials and equipment and from manufacturing and payroll expenses.

Boiled down, the governmental spending on infrastructure is enormous, but the money can (and should) go to all communities. Traditionally, more affluent communities and municipalities have benefitted from "new" infrastructure at the expense of underrepresented communities. There has been some shifting of the overall benefits recently. Still, it's been more of a philosophical shift than a seismic shift felt by those who need the infrastructure improvements and all they entail (jobs, housing, business growth) the most. Only you, your local neighbors, and politicians can guarantee that your community benefits from spending dollars across the country.

The best way to start is to employ the heart and soul of *Bridging Capital for Impact.*

Private Sector and Public Sector Financing

Goals for transforming your business into a community-enhancing enterprise or managing an infrastructure-based project should all start with a feasibility study. As fancy and intimidating as that might sound, it's nothing more than looking at the practicality of your ideas and project. And you can start by simply thinking deeply about your plans or brainstorming with friends.

Taking notes can strengthen your commitment to the project, and listing ideas, strengths, and weaknesses inherent in such an undertaking will give you some ideas about the path you will be taking. Ideally, your plans will eventually include the costs you'll incur and the value you can reasonably expect to attain.

Remember that the value you are trying to achieve may be more than just financial. Still, from a practical viewpoint, those offering to finance usually need to be reassured that their investment will be rewarded. In most cases, infrastructure finance is considered a long-term loan, usually secured by land, buildings, and asset cash flows.

Financing may come from all sectors of the P4s, but your emphasis may be predetermined depending on your business model or structure. We'll dig deeper into those considerations in later sections, but for now, be aware that a business model dependent on third parties will likely have more significant cash flow risks than those that rely on revenues provided directly by the government. The same will likely be true for procurement options.

If your project is for the public sector, the government may provide funding at the project level or finance at the government level, where the government borrows the funds and provides them for your project.

In most cases, the government provides funding for a specific project (often interest-free or as a grant), or the funding comes through a CDFI investment. However, when a private sector business such as a bank provides capital, there will be a repayment schedule.

In either case, you'll have spent much time and filled multiple pages detailing your project; your initial, interim, and ending financial needs; and the business model your project will follow. That set of documents and financials will underscore your business, your associates, your proposal's potential risks, when your costs will be incurred, and when any revenues will begin to offset any costs.

As for cash flow, the exact sources of revenue can determine the level of risk associated with your project. For example, suppose your revenues will be funded by the government and spread over the life of your building/project/asset. In that case, there will likely be reduced risk in the cost of finance – instead of up-front capital expenditure for assets used over many years.

Funding may come from public and private sources, but your financials and projections must emphasize enough free cash flow to repay the loans approved by the private sector.

Public sector (government) investment may generate direct value through usage fees such as bridge tolls and indirect value by generating land value increases similar outcomes. Private sector investment may be spurred by some of the attractive characteristics of infrastructure financials, which include these:

- Stability—especially true for public use projects exhibiting predictable cash flow
- Steady Cash Flow—continuous when projects have contracted revenue models
- Nonseasonal—noncyclical projects such as utilities are not impacted by inflation
- High Usage—once paid for, small marginal per-use costs and low variability
- High Leverage—stable cash flow results in high levels of financing leverage

Still, there are always risks involved with any project, even those that are infrastructure related. The positive high leverage that can be obtained can backfire, as highly leveraged projects result in high financing costs (interest).

In addition, local infrastructure projects, especially if they involve any type of public domain recapture, will disrupt the social community of the area. Change is difficult and frightening for many people, even when it is for the public good. In addition, there is always an ESG risk, the public interpretation of environmental, social, and governance issues created by any changes. The larger the project, the more the study necessary to anticipate and dissipate public usage disruption.

Often private sector financing will be a mix of debt and equity. The bank or fund takes a reduced risk by holding a mortgage against physical assets or an income stream. The form of the mix or split will depend on how the investor views the project's viability and overall risk, as will the cost of capital.

Subordinated debt may be used and repaid after the senior debt is exhausted. In this case, the percentage of senior debt available will be high in lower-risk projects but considerably less in higher-risk deals.

The financing type varies depending on the lenders' view of the project's cost and repayment methods. Financing is usually split into either debt or equity.

Debt financing is usually the choice for government projects (since we'll assume the government isn't shutting down shortly). This funding limits the lender's return to interest earned on the principal and repayment. The debt always has a maturity date, so both the lender and borrower know precisely when the loan will be paid in full. Loan periods of one year or less are known as short-term. Long-term debt is structured over more than one year.

Interest, principal, and rates are spelled out with a provision specifying how and when the interest and principal shall be paid. In addition, some loans may include grace periods to allow the borrower to postpone payments until the project has positive cash flow.

As noted earlier, Seniority is the factor determining the highest rights and first claim to the income and assets of the business. Only when those claims are satisfied do subordinate debt holders receive payment.

Debt can be obtained on a secured or unsecured basis, but is usually issued with no security beyond the cash flows and assets. Fixed-rate loans don't change. Floating rates may be tied to a lender's prime or US prime rates.

Equity financing is often the choice when investors take shares of the project's business in exchange for their capital. The capital need not be cash and can come from sponsors, private investors, government, or internally generated (from partners). Equity financing is often a long-term investment and is subject to change on the basis of a mutual agreement in the future.

While debt financing provides loan and interest payments, equity financing provides dividends and capital gains when net earnings allow. This gives equity holders a chance to get total returns in the future.

Should the borrower default, debt holders are the first to claim the borrower's income and assets toward settling the debt. However, should the company stay afloat, equity holders have unlimited potential returns—generated cash.

Financing Stages

Before financing, it's also essential for the borrower to look at the stages of infrastructure construction. In the early stages, the project has been taken from the boardroom or blackboard state to a point where financials have been verified, stakeholders have been identified, and locations have been identified, perhaps even secured via purchase or lease option.

Plans are drawn but are preliminary. Any attempt to obtain financing will likely be unsuccessful as the project is most at risk during this stage.

In the middle stages, more exact plans have been verified, stakeholders have signed on to the overall project plans, and environmental studies may be sanctioned or already have been conducted. Financing risk here is lower, but without specific assets such as land ownership and other guarantees, interest rates offered may still be high.

Later stages of development can be represented by the purchased land, buildings, and businesses already operating and generating revenue. An example could be a mass transit project—a bus line— where the buses ran, revenue came in, and risk was lowest.

As discussed, financing may come from public or private entities and be debt or equity. Blended finance may also be used when public funds fund only a portion of the investment. Private sources sometimes fund the remaining investment, but it may also come from philanthropies.

The final stage of financing a project is researching every available avenue adequately and precisely to define the appropriate delivery mechanism. As always, projects, financials, and all business overview details should be transparent to all parties, and all contracts should be verified and approved by experienced attorneys. Taking local input from politicians and city planners is also wise.

The final preparation should include a study of all possible outcomes and include the consideration of factors like risk, management, and future challenges. Bringing together public and private funding may be a crucial part of a project, but don't expect the government to be better prepared than the private sector. Guarantees are rarely fool-proof, even when carefully worded in agreements and contracts. Nothing verbal should be considered.

Do the MATH — Momentum Always Trumps Hesitation

Private Sector Participation

When it comes to infrastructure investment, there are many reasons that the collaboration of public and private sector funding is necessary. Still, the major one is that infrastructure investment as a percentage of the Gross Domestic Product has fallen in the US over the past decade. Both local and federal representatives talk a good game about investing in infrastructure, but often, the costs don't seem to fit into state and federal budgets.

Voters tend to ask, "What have you done for me lately?" of their politicians, and spending large sums of money on long-term projects isn't sexy. Traffic disruptions, dust, increased truck traffic, and earthmoving equipment trying to navigate snarled intersections have a negative twist. Those issues tend to stop or delay large projects, but money is still significant. Therefore, increased Private Sector Participation (PSP) can be the key to achieving public sector objectives.

On the other side, local businesses see the need for community change, which may or may not include infrastructure changes, but they, and you, can drive the government to understand how vital specific local projects are to the people they will support. Additionally, forces are driving the need for more spending, including growth, urbanization, and new technology.

Growing up in a rural community has increased many people's sense of security and community. Still, the community stagnates when there's no usable internet bandwidth, no fiber-optic lines, and no room to grow. Expanding municipalities need investment in critical areas like schools, libraries, hospitals, emergency services, and family-need outlets like grocery stores, pharmacies, and banks.

It is getting increasingly difficult to find funding for roads, bridges, and water systems. Still, the private sector can lead the way by developing community projects and increasing their lending practices to include more local businesses to detail, supply, and build necessary services.

Infrastructure that has been traditionally financed through tax-exempt and taxable bonds is seeing more TIRZs, opportunity zone credits, value capture, user fees, and even privatization. These incentives give local businesses with P4 goals a better chance to be involved in neighborhood and regional projects that can transform communities.

As mentioned earlier, the value capture can be generated directly or indirectly and is usually enjoyed by the government. However, private firms can employ the same methodology and capture the difference between early land/structure value and the increase after improvements. This "capture of value" benefits the business by increasing the project's overall value and reducing the financing percentage to book value.

Swaps and asset recycling can also enhance the private sector when the government owns assets that aren't generating as much (if any) income as they could. For example, swapping equal-value pieces of land, say one in an industrial area for one in a non-commercial area, could help a private firm obtain a spot to generate revenue.

The government can also sell assets to private firms for its general fund or turn around and use the revenue to begin additional infrastructure projects, helping both sides move forward.

U.S. Bank has committed to supporting communities with economic inequities to create lasting change. The bank's initiative is an excellent study of how financial institutions view the importance of their partners and the importance of promoting sustainability and stability in local cities.

The bank recognizes that every community has unique needs and will have local community affairs managers offer invitations to the grant program to nonprofit organizations. In addition, new organizations may submit a letter of interest found on their website.

A unique feature of the program is an emphasis (grant categories) on play (arts, culture, places to play), work (workforce education and economic prosperity), and home (neighborhood stability and revitalization). All organizations must have IRS tax-exempt status—Section 501(c)(3).

Their other requirements mirror specifics that other financial institutions are likely to require:

- Daily Operations Grants—cover most ongoing expenses, including salaries
- Project Grants—cover expenses of specific activities with a predetermined cost and clear start and end dates
- Capital Grants—cover the purchase (finance) of fixed assets

The best part of the U.S. Bank's grant program is that it directly infuses capital into communities in need and various areas often overlooked by traditional investments. Areas like arts, culture, and places to play help neighborhoods create their theme or culture and create pride. I firmly believe a family should not have to leave their community, in search of community.

> **No two people experience reality the same because we individually create it internally.**

CHAPTER TWELVE:
Live, Learn, and Lead

It's easy to decide whether we want to change the world or our little part of heaven. It's much harder to check off the many steps necessary to invoke that change because change comes with uncertainty, for good or bad.

Well, who knows, but as social activist and folksinger Pete Seeger once said, and I'm paraphrasing, *"At the end of the day, whether we helped enact change or not, I'd rather spend my time with the activists than with their detractors."*

Sometimes it takes a Herculean effort to enact the changes we'd all like to see, but the flip side is doing nothing and living with the consequences. Governments have the same uncertainty issues as private citizens because they are made up of the same groups—people with many questions and too few answers. That's also why infrastructure is often so complex for the public sector to handle successfully.

Without denigrating the government (too much), the private sector is competent in discerning what the public (the people) wants and needs. And the private sector excels at financing practices mandatory for large projects. Public-private partnership (PPP) requires interdisciplinary business development skills—from finance, accounting, and taxes—to general economics, engineering, and social-environ-mental disciplines. Both sides contribute.

Still, without buy-in from the government, PPPs are complex and can be doomed to failure. Handling all processes in cooperation, not competition, is often the key. And while many citizens think of governments as rich, only about 16 percent of governments worldwide can fund their infrastructure projects without private investment.

It has been economically slothful in the US to put off upgrading our crumbling infrastructure (ports, highways, bridges). Still, it has been done because getting "additional funding" approved in any legislature is complex and can lead to problems with reelection. Of course, it is the same with social security, but that's another story.

As for other necessary infrastructure at more local levels, upgrading fiber optic cables has been an ongoing fight in many communities. More changes to include innovative technology will lead to more fights. Who pays the bill? Ultimately, the taxpayers and consumers—as always. But your vision for change in your community can be transformational if you use your voice and incorporate the *Bridging Capital for Impact* model.

If you have ideas or plans for *Bridging Capital for Impact*, use some of the cornerstones of the P4s in your efforts, whether they include the private sector or a PPP.

- Due Diligence—Before considering a business plan or feasibility study, start with a list of goals. Then move on to achieving those goals before considering your plan's impact on your community. If the changes are suitable for everyone, you shouldn't be afraid to discuss your plans with others. Only then can you be sure you've got sound ideas. If you do, everyone in your group will understand the goals of your project as well as the financial considerations and the planning necessary to bring it to fruition

- Anticipate Change—Whether personally or as a PPP; business partnerships can fail if officials don't anticipate the inevitable changes, such as the loss of valuable stakeholders, funding, land or facility use, or public sentiment. Partners must be proactive instead of reactive. To do so, absolute transparency is necessary for everyone involved. There should be no secrets in the board room, and contingency or backup plans should always be available
- Buy-in—Your partners should all have ultimate buy-in for the project. Your shared vision should be twenty-twenty. Shortsighted or myopic vision is a huge liability. If your project is a PPP, remember that both sectors have specific agendas that must share the ultimate goals for the community. Don't assume; make sure your development team has the right expertise. Developers new to the public-private arena tend to underestimate the importance of adding specialized expertise to their development team. Depending on the project, that can range from members skilled in facilitating public dialogue to municipal advisors, bond counsel, and redevelopment counsel. If the developer is new to the community, it's wise to add local expertise, focusing on those who offer insight and experience with the public partner
- Mutual Trust—Knowing your partner's strengths and weaknesses will keep you on an even keel in all business settings. Motivation is necessary for every partnership, but the government answers to a larger constituency than the private sector. They move slower and aren't as interested in

the profits and bottom line the private sector need to see to move forward

- Allocation of Funds—The public sector or specific stakeholders may need to ensure that they haven't allocated more funds than necessary for a responsible and adequate business deal. Both parties must feel they've been negotiated with in good faith and reached a fair agreement. Don't demand the fruits of the art of the deal; arrive at a compromise that shows the mutual respect partners need
- Realistic Timelines—Don't overestimate your ability to finish a project in record time. Trust your planners, contractors, and partners to provide realistic timelines for each phase of your project
- Constant Contact—Keep your partners well-informed at all times. Accept debate and compromise as equitable business practices and build transparent processes for all phases of planning, implementing, and documenting your project's building and running phases. Although some businesses can tragically drown in paperwork,
  all parties must have access to critical information at any time

If you can dream, you can prepare and gain support; you can gain traction in your goals to make transformational change in your community and your life!

When my aunt passed away in the city I was raised in, I traveled back home to New York, but I didn't stay in my old neighborhood. I decided not to crash on the couch at my buddy's place. Instead, I checked into a hotel room downtown. I purposely didn't stay in the old neighborhood because although times have changed, the crime rate remains high.

Instead of me hanging out on the block, a few of my neighborhood friends showed up at my hotel, and we enjoyed a box of Masculino Premium Cigars and reminisced about life.

I purposely created a different experience to enjoy my time there. I pulled them into my reality versus returning to the neighborhood.

I did this not because I felt I was "better than the block" but because the effect of doing so could empower others to set higher expectations from themselves, help them see more, know more, and do better.

One person can make an impact, and I have witnessed this from sitting on both sides of the table. That's just a reality of life as we build and grow. So instead of me going back, my old friends showed up at my hotel, and we all shared a cigar and conversation.

Give yourself room to be wrong... It helps you to become wiser in a shorter period of time.

SECTION FOUR

CHAPTER THIRTEEN:
The Role of the Philanthropic Sector

You don't have to be a foundation to give charitably to others, whether it's something you drop in the collection plate at church or indirectly support a cause by buying cookies. Giving to a worthy cause can make you feel good (even without the cookies) and spur hope while encouraging others to share their charity.

Philanthropy usually involves giving on a larger scale than most can afford. It is usually tied to a group or organization wishing to help humankind significantly. And as many foundations prove, giving time and effort can be a charitable act that makes a noticeable change in the world. And then there's a not-so-minor thing called tax benefits that can prod some affluent givers to cough up the cash. And that's a good thing.

Philanthropy aims high, with sights set on social changes, renovating blighted areas, designating scholarships for decades to come, and changing the course of humanity. It's a big deal with huge goals. Often, those goals are achieved through the efforts of the many, not the few.

To drive that point home, let me say that it is estimated that individuals gave an estimated $350 billion in charity in 2021, while corporations gave an estimated $21 billion. There is power in the masses, and working together toward goals, even against formidable challenges, can have excellent results.

A Little Philanthropic History

There are direct historical accounts of philanthropy dating back at least several thousand years. For example, it is said that the Greek philosopher Plato asked his nephew in 347 BC to sell the family farm and give the proceeds to a teaching facility Plato had founded.

In the US, John Harvard bequeathed half his estate in 1638 to found Harvard University. Today the college is one of the highest-ranking and has the largest endowment at $42 billion. Harvard not only teaches thousands of students each year, but their research labs in many fields also provide a place for students and scholars to test and verify theories that have led to significant advances.

While John Harvard's actions benefited students mostly at one location, industrialist Andrew Carnegie used his wealth to start and support several universities. In addition, his foundation has helped build more than 2,500 libraries all over the world.

In 2022, I attended the Harvard Kennedy School. Twelve months later, I completed and obtained the Public Leadership Credentials (PLC) certificate. This exemplifies my passion and commitment to bridging capital into undercapitalized communities.

Many artists have donated time and money to causes they feel passionate about in the entertainment industry. Musician Alicia Keyes co-founded *the Keep A Child Alive Foundation* nearly twenty years ago and continues to donate her time and money to other charitable causes. Basketball star David "The Admiral" Robinson pledged $9 million to build and operate the Carver Academy in San Antonio.

Michael Jackson donated his musical efforts and more than $100 million to various foundations.

And then there's Oprah Winfrey. Oprah has delighted, encouraged, and inspired millions of viewers as a producer, actress, and talk show host. And as a philanthropist, she has led the way in making change a reality for millions of in-need recipients.

The Oprah Winfrey Charitable Foundation's words:

Oprah has long believed that education is the door to freedom, offering a chance at a brighter future. Through her private charity, she has awarded hundreds of grants to organizations that support the education and empowerment of women, children, and families in the United States and around the world. Among her various philanthropic contributions, she has donated millions of dollars toward providing a better education for students with merit but no means. "The Oprah Winfrey Scholars Program" was created to give scholarships to students determined to use their education to give back to their communities in the United States and abroad.

The foundation's work is astonishing, especially in the critical areas of food insecurity and education. While donating over $400 million to change the world, the OWCF has educated seventy-two thousand students and served seventy-five million meals. Those numbers speak for themselves.

There are a still wider variety of philanthropic organizations. Some are small, local groups focusing on community philanthropy, and others are global and tremendously funded, like the IKEA Foundation with a $65 billion endowment. Considering which is the best would be disingenuous since a detailed tracking of every group would take years. However, with publicity and longevity, some organizations do stand out.

The Bill and Melinda Gates Foundation has garnered news for many reasons, but they encapsulate their foundation as "A nonprofit fighting poverty, disease, and inequity worldwide." It's a noble goal.

In their 2020 year-end report, they boasted that their 1,357 grantees received $5.8 billion in direct support. It's a staggering amount, and the foundation employs more than 1,700 people. Since 2000, the foundation has spent $53.8 billion. Again, a staggering amount.

Some studies show that charitable giving can improve one's emotional and physical well-being. As a result, philanthropists may live longer than those who don't give to their fellow populists.

Heading toward his ninety-second birthday this year, Warren Buffet has donated the most money (ever, by anyone).

> **She is great not because she has not failed.**
> **She is great because failure did not stop her.**

CHAPTER FOURTEEN:

Yesterday's Challenges, Tomorrow's Opportunities

Perhaps the most exciting part of Sharkey's article mentioned in Chapter Three is the notion of a "community quarterback" being situated in every low-income neighborhood. This isn't necessarily a person—it is much more likely an organization. The community of East Lake in Atlanta, Georgia, was transformed mainly due to the *Purpose-Built Communities* organization (purposebuiltcommunities.org), an institution that "took ownership over the community and responsibility for all of the residents within it."

Thus, the organization successfully functioned as the "community quarterback." The article suggests that federal resources should be combined with resources from foundations and the private sector to identify or establish a community quarterback in every low-income community across the country. This way, "everyone within that neighborhood knows an institution is serving them for the long haul and will have sufficient resources to bring about long-term change."

This concept is very much a part of the P4 initiative, although the more common term used under the initiative is "community partner." We'll also look at an affiliated term: "community development officer."

A Local Example

In 2020, I sat on the regional economic development committee that hosted a conference filled with prestigious and forward-thinking guests in Houston. We focused on one particular issue that affects everyone, everywhere—the revitalization of local economies. Hands down, revitalization should be a significant priority of community leaders and government officials, business owners, consumers, and taxpayers. Of course, we all want to thrive where we are planted, and many do just that. But not all.

Some exist, or perhaps just survive, in blighted neighborhoods similar to the neighborhood I was raised in—a community with limited access to capital. My neighborhood received the barest amount of investment, definitely not enough to impact change or tap the potential of the citizens living there. I was fortunate to graduate from high school and even more fortunate to go to college, where I witnessed the chasm between social classes.

The fact was that we had no community partners to assist in impact investment.

The definition of a community partner varies widely and depends on context. According to San Jose State University, "Community partners are nonprofit organizations, public agencies, government offices, schools, and certain private businesses where students provide community service as an integral part of their academic courses."

Indiana University—Bloomington defines community partners with the following quote: "A community partner may be, but is not limited to, the following: local, state, national, international, public, community-based, private and academic organization. Partnerships will promote student engagement, workforce development, continuing education, community service, and collaborative and community-based research."

The Texas Community Partner Program (www.texascommunitypartnerprogram.com/) "builds bridges between Texas Health and Human Services and Texas communities to provide Texans access to food, cash, and health care." The program supports partner organizations through dedicated regional support staff, information sharing, direct access to HHS, and much more. Partners receive support, training, certification, resources, feedback opportunities, and increased visibility.

While I'm pleased that these institutions attach an academic and healthcare component (high concentrations of crucial "eds and meds" regional benefit growth), my definition focuses on the financial aspect, public policy, and business backdrop. For instance, the Greater Houston Partnership "works hand-in-hand with the partnership policy committee members, board members, elected officials and outside organizations as a regional facilitator for issues affecting the business community." In addition, it helps facilitate international investment and trade initiatives.

The Financial Perspective

A community partner is an intermediary and links investment fund managers with the community's economic development area from a financial perspective. The community partner ensures that the determined social goals and population and employment density factors are realized.

Frankly, the cities of the twenty-first century require inner-city assets, as inner-city population density supports regional retail, personal service, and other investments. Inner-city employment density facilitates communication, knowledge spillovers, and innovation that drives competitiveness in the US. Both factors require transportation infrastructure assets within the inner city, and Houston traffic is no exception (perhaps a topic for a different time).

In short, the community partner is the "face of the faceless" (the people in the P4 paradigm) and is in tune with the dynamics within any given community. The community partner assesses the financial needs and presents impact investment opportunities to the other P4 partners—the public, private and philanthropic sectors.

PRIs and MRIs (Program & Mission Related Investments)

As mentioned, our nation is an extraordinary example of generosity by any world standard. I believe this is driven by the culture of charity rooted in our churches and encouraged through tax advantages. Even with the new tax law, philanthropic giving and social investing are encouraged.

The US treasury department has made it easier for private foundations to achieve more significant charitable outcomes through investment returns by which endowments are grown. Impact investors work with foundations to leverage these funds through program-related investments (PRIs) and mission-related investments (MRIs)—sometimes referred to as "mission" investments and "double-line" investments. They are vehicles through which individuals, corporations, and philanthropies can effect change on behalf of the underserved—with certain caveats.

According to the IRS, the primary purpose of PRIs is to accomplish one or more of the foundation's exempt purposes and significantly further the foundation's exempt activities. Examples include the following:

- Low-interest or interest-free loans to needy students
- High-risk investments in nonprofit low-income housing projects
- Low-interest loans to small businesses owned by members of economically disadvantaged groups, where commercial funds at reasonable interest rates are not readily available
- Investments in businesses in low-income areas (both domestic and foreign) under a plan to improve the economy of the area by providing employment or training for unemployed residents
- Investments in nonprofit organizations combating community deterioration

Similar to PRIs, MRIs can be an investment where the intention is to earn both a social and a financial return but are not designed to meet the IRS requirements to qualify as a PRI. In May 2019, the Cleveland Foundation recently announced an expansion in the money it earmarks for its social impact investing, saying that it would allocate $150 million in capital by the end of 2022 As part of the overall impact investment goal of $150 million, the foundation hopes to more than double the amount it currently invests in MRIs and recoverable grants by 2022.

The Rockefeller Foundation is a prime example. In 2013, the foundation released a book titled "The Power of Impact Investing: Putting Markets to Work for Profit and Global Good" that examines the potential of impact investing on the structures, systems, and practices needed to make it "go big and go global." They identified the need for better data sharing among impact investors and better systems for evaluating impact investments. The foundation released a comprehensive independent twelve-year evaluation of its Program-Related Investment (PRI) Fund conducted by Arabella Advisors, including eighteen transactions totaling $23.9 million domestically and internationally to assess the portfolio's social and financial performance as well as opportunities to refine the PRI program strategy and align it with the foundation's focus areas and grant-making programs.

The Rockefeller Foundation's PRIs have contributed to the financial sustainability of investees and are helping them accomplish social goals, achieve impact, help excluded populations access products and services on more equitable terms and in new ways, and increase the number and quality of jobs in the United States, Mexico, India, and East Africa. When investees noted that staff development and leadership training were crucial to successful program implementation, the Rockefeller Foundation reconsidered how to use both grants and investments to support the same organization and also how grant funding can complement PRIs and other impact investments to support organizations that are helping the poor, the vulnerable, and the environment.

The Bill and Melinda Gates Foundation is another example of PRIs in action. In 2013, the foundation made a PRI in the Nairobi-based for-profit startup M-KOPA, which sells solar lighting and mobile phone charging systems on a pay-as-you-go basis to East African households. They did so in partnership with a local commercial bank so that M-KOPA could develop a credit history and attract future commercial lenders. The foundation's loan was accompanied by a grant to support new product development and expansion into new geographic areas.

In 2014, the Gates Foundation made a $20 million equity investment in Kymab Ltd. based in Cambridge, England. Despite being sued for patent infringement, the company had promising technology that made it ideal for early-stage venture capital funding. The Gates Foundation did its due diligence and found the risk was balanced by the opportunity to secure reliable access to future drugs and vaccines that could be delivered for affordable prices in developing countries. By the end of 2014, the foundation had committed $3.65 million in targeted research grants and other biotech equity investments.

In 2016 the Gates Foundation also allocated $1.5 billion to fund PRIs, enabling the foundation to reach beyond the nonprofit sector and draw on the talent, expertise, and innovations offered by the private sector to advance its mission to "help all people lead healthy, productive lives." The foundation invested in scaling up enterprises that serve the poor and guaranteeing public agencies' purchases of vaccines and contraceptive implants to convince large pharmaceutical manufacturers that they should boost their production and reduce prices for those most in need.

What Works Cities

The Bloomberg Philanthropies' approach, in part, entails the "What Works Cities" program (part of the American Cities Initiative) that "empowers cities to generate innovation and advance policy that moves the nation forward" through data and evidence-based decision-making. Interestingly, in 2018, Bloomberg's American Cities Initiative made a novel effort to examine city leaders' issues "from the heartland to the high-rise." The most comprehensive public opinion survey resulted in a multi-topic survey of mayors and city managers.

The survey included data gathered from large, medium, and small cities in the Midwest, Northeast, South, and West regions. Although the bulk of the report focused on policy concerns like climate change, the opioid crisis, and managing growth, it also included a "Thinking Ahead" section in which mayors weighed in on what they thought was the biggest problem for the country in ten years.

Surprisingly—and perhaps disappointingly from an impact investment standpoint—only 15 percent of the mayors cited inequality, or the widening rift between the haves and have-nots, as a significant issue facing communities in the future.

When surveyed about "Room for Improvement," 25 percent responded with "jobs and economic growth," and 20 percent cited "affordable housing." This may indicate that the genuine issues of urban decay and undercapitalization are not adequately addressed. Worse, it may indicate that the voice of the marginalized is not being heard or that the marginalized have not been able to garner the attention of their elected officials.

In my opinion, the survey's lack of focus on bridging capital to undercapitalized communities is both a lesson and an opportunity to do better. Impact investors and community partners must include mayors, city managers, and city councils in the planning and preparation phases of bridging capital initiatives.

Community Philanthropy

The idea of community philanthropy certainly isn't a new concept. Ancient civilizations practiced community survival methods, and while sharing resources wasn't always equal, each person and family unit that contributed to the community pool was able to survive. In Native American society, each tribe worked for the greater good of the people. Their pooling and sharing of resources protected the community.

Fast-forwarding through the years to the twenty-first century, we find that the US became a land of the haves and the have-nots. Much of the disparity in wealth had not to do with ability but with opportunity, education, and nationality. The American landscape was dotted with towns surrounded by thousands of acres of land, while the hub of growth and prosperity followed traditional trails and trading outposts and waterways. Those locations were composed of new emigrants—most of whom spoke little to no English—forced to live in squalor and despair with no heat, running water, or hope.

New York, Chicago, and Philadelphia dominated the country population-wise, but two Ohio cities, Cleveland, and Cincinnati, were in the top ten. Columbus and Toledo weren't far behind. And nothing was more evident than the simple fact that poverty was rampant, and the educational system was in tragic shape. The larger the town, the worse the poverty and disparity of income and opportunity. As the country grew at an astonishing pace, complex challenges resulted from the industrialization and urban sprawl that segmented society to even greater degrees.

To fulfil the demand for workers, companies across the US hired children—as young as nine or ten years old—to work ten-hour days for as little as six cents per hour. Then, in 1906, Upton Sinclair's *The Jungle* was published, exposing the exploitation of American factory workers while highlighting the meatpacking industry of Chicago's slaughterhouses.

Although Sinclair later admitted his celebrity arose "not because the public cared anything about the workers, but simply because the public did not want to eat tubercular beef," many people knew things needed to change.

Those people included the mayor of Cleveland, Ohio, Tom L. Johnson. He represented the ideals of the Progressive movement and fought to counter the strength of big businesses and bring assistance to those struggling mightily to manage their meager incomes. He also supported the municipal ownership of public utilities and battled the city's streetcar companies—along with Cleveland lawyer Frederick H. Goff—to lower the fare to three cents.

Later, Goff was hired by the Cleveland Trust Company, which had plans to become the "people's bank." Goff took a pay cut since he was inspired by what he saw as the opportunity to make drastic civic changes as the bank's full-time president.

After five years of exemplary work, Goff convinced the bank to adopt a Resolution and Declaration of Trust to create a new organization—the Cleveland Foundation.

"The Cleveland Foundation's mission is to enhance the lives of all residents of Greater Cleveland, now and for generations to come, by working together with our donors to build community endowment, address needs through grant-making, and provide leadership on key community issues."

Once the five-member grant-making body was finalized, Goff announced that the community trust would undertake "a great social and economic survey of Cleveland to uncover the causes of poverty and crime and point out the cure."

The research initiatives targeting public education, recreation, and criminal justice stirred public indignation while garnering extensive press coverage that helped goad the city and the state of Ohio to take notice.

Since then, the Cleveland Foundation has inspired hundreds of community foundations, twelve of which were established in 1915 alone. Grants given by the Cleveland Foundation total billions of dollars. In 2020 the value of the grants authorized by them was $124 million.

Goff's idea of searching for the root cause of community failings and struggles helped kick off the Cleveland Foundation's success. Today, many groups have replicated his efforts by gaining the support of community members and finding external resources (grants, loans, tax incentives, income opportunities) to meet challenges and improve residents' quality of life.

Community Participation

In practice, even at the grassroots level, community participation comes with trust, and collaboration with the public, private, and philanthropic sectors is greatly enhanced when decision-making is shared at all levels. Trust and support start with ideas and plans for the community from the knowledge and experience of locals from all walks of life.

In-kind contributions can kick-start efforts to meet and greet (food and beverage, meeting space), and tools and equipment can help physical building efforts. While cash contributions are always helpful, pro bono services are welcome contributions toward lodging, meals, tax and legal help, and sponsorships.

For local community coordinators and organizers, local philanthropy is a great start. The P4s include the participation of people in the community, and bridging capital often starts with a single person's ideas for improvement.

With local efforts, community members have absolute control over their dreams' direction since they have a unique knowledge of what has transpired over the years and what needs to be addressed for a strong future. And while outside pressures may be evident, the residents can provide the ultimate commitment for time, connections, and history.

Because of these factors, building trust (and building a sustainable job base and assets) is best handled through community philanthropy initiatives and local input—although the influx of bridging capital is often necessary. It is the empowerment of the people, the individuals, and groups that find their voice and become active players that make community participation a wonderful, encouraging, and powerful thing.

Those same groups become accountable for their ideas and actions and the implementation of goals necessary to revitalize blighted areas. Their work actively facilitates an increase in local identification and bridging capital.

Actual change cannot be sustained without a local platform. Sustainability is always in question without a long-term approach, constant care, and local oversight. Community foundations that constantly monitor progress and are there to adjust programs and keep them evolving have much greater success than groups championing change from afar.

According to the Council on Foundations, more than 750 grant-making public charities—community foundations—operate in urban and rural areas of the United States. They support disaster relief, environmental causes, health and human services, and arts and education fields. In 2017 alone, those foundations granted nearly $5.48 billion.

Community Philanthropy Models:

- Community Foundation—receives funds from diverse sources and often participates in geographic areas through grant-making as a public charity

- Giving Circles—pool resources between friends and like-minded individuals with local needs as their primary goal
- Youth Banks—originally started in the 1990s in the UK to help young people create organized savings for grant-giving—most often aimed at overlooked and underappreciated activities older citizens aren't addressing
- Identity-based—designed to promote philanthropy targeted at specific groups (religious federations, children's groups, women's funds, library initiatives) and causes
- Community-Driven Development—the community or "beneficiaries" have participation, if not always "control," from idea to implementation, evaluation, and overall guidance for targeting support toward critical issues within often marginalized communities

Community philanthropy doesn't always need to follow a model since any effort to address local issues is a noble goal. Whether it starts or ends, the chance to induce bridging capital to communities is worth the work.

You can become as small as your controlling desire or as great as your dominant aspiration.

CHAPTER FIFTEEN:

Put Your Money Where Your Mouth Is

Fortunately, the government is evolving positively and today provides a broad spectrum of funding solutions for *Bridging Capital for Impact* and designing programs that work well for under-resourced and underrepresented communities. How each works best with your implementation plans could fill another book, but that's one you'll have to write after the incredible journey you take in changing your world.

Since this book is written to inspire and expand the flow of capital into communities, there is an emphasis on community philanthropy. And it is indeed exciting to say that this field is moving forward at a pace it never has before. Of course, social media is responsible for some of that growth, but dare I say that the world is growing a conscience about minority issues, whether that minority is race or income based? Perhaps.

Regardless of the history and future of community philanthropy, the status quo is no longer an acceptable option. Thousands of communities are in flux, ready for change, awaiting strong leaders and financial backing.

Challenging the old regime is a time-honored tradition of forward-looking people, and nothing is more important right now than aligning our priorities and putting them into action. With the right tools, we can all be part of the solution and witness historical change!

Collaboration and innovation are critical parts of the successful transformation of the blighted and undermanaged areas of our country. Community foundations are perfect entities for forming small and large-scale partnerships with national corporations and government agencies. Along the way, those foundations can learn from other successful joint ventures. It's not necessary to reinvent the wheel. It's only essential that we follow the example of the wheels that run smoothly without crashing.

Given that thinking, perhaps someday, those foundations can join forces as a network of groups across a county, state, or even the whole US. But before we get there, let's consider funding solutions to fuel our dreams of bridging capital to locally and regionally-focused organizations.

Often overlooked funding solutions for community organizations include these:

- Civic Clubs—Civic associations allow members to converse with local government officials or others within the community. Examples include the League of Women Voters, the Lions Club, the Fraternal Order of Eagles, CORE, and the National Urban League
- Charitable Gift Funds (CGFs)—A CGF is created to manage charitable donations on behalf of an individual or family. It is often called a Commercial Charitable Gift Fund if it represents
  an organization

- Community Foundation Funds (CFFs)—Keeping grants and funding local is the goal of CFFs, which aim to bring communities together to discuss social challenges and opportunities in the region
- Crowdfunding—Online gifts provided for individuals and organizations, most often for charitable or social causes, is what crowdfunding aims to facilitate
- Direct Giving—Many people give direct funds to charitable causes, especially if the organizational recipient is nonprofit and community-based
- Giving Circles—This is a dynamic way for people with shared values to pool their time and money for proactive change and civic action
- Giving Federations—Many giving federations are philanthropic groups like CARE and UNICEF that provide necessary "gifts" for survival. Doctors without Borders is one that provides more than sustenance, while others like the Give Foundation provide education, environmental sustainability, and entrepreneurship funding to drive lasting, positive change in communities
- Identity-Based Funds—These solicit community contributions and redistribute those funds as grants to local individuals and organizations working to promote social change
- Religious Organizations—Churches and religious orders often raise funds for local causes that champion community change
- Private Foundations—It's not just Philanthropic Foundations that grant money to drive change. Private foundations, categorized as private operating foundations that run the charitable activities or organizations they fund with their

investment income and private nonoperating foundations that disburse funds to other charitable organizations, provide much-needed grants and charitable donations to communities and organizations in need

- Public Foundations—Most charitable organizations, such as the NAACP and the American Red Cross, are public foundations. Organizations such as the Public Welfare Foundation provide support in many justice areas and provide grants directly
- Single Issue Charity—Single-issue nonprofits are tax-exempt groups organized around a specific topic, such as faith, identity, or cause. They often gift (grant) issue-specific nonprofits focused on communities, the environment, and health and social justice. In addition, some funds focus on specific groups of people such as women and girls, people of color, the LGBTQ community, etc.

Funding can also come from investment funds tailored to social inequity, social responsibility, sustainable power, etc. As investors, individuals can put their dollars to work in managed funds that support causes they, too, support and can even find local funds ready to provide capital for the very communities.

The organizations undertaking the social change or capital improvements raise money for their community from investors and the many funding solutions listed previously. Or they can be funded—in part or whole—by a Community Investment Fund (CIF). The beauty of a CIF is that even people of modest means can impact the project's success by investing in it.

When the investments make sound changes, a healthy cycle of revitalization, growth, profit, and reinvestment benefits the community and the investors. As the CIF grows, so does its ability to reapply profits into new ventures.

Diversification stabilizes the CIF and makes it more scalable as funds are reinvested. Larger projects are then possible as the fund can continue to raise money for new ventures. CIFs can be categorized into charitable loan funds, real estate revitalization funds, and diversified business funds.

A charitable loan fund is exempt from the fundamental federal securities laws and invests in ventures most aligned with a nonprofit's vision.

A real estate revitalization fund is designed for community repair and change. In most cases, the fund raises capital to purchase and revitalize commercial and residential properties for later sale or lease. The fund may offer investors equity, debt, or revenue share securities, and profits may be distributed among investors.

A diversified business fund has several distinct advantages. Although the fund can't invest more than 40 percent of its assets in "investment securities," it can offer investors an equity position in the business that manages the fund. Afterward, the fund can take equity positions in other businesses.

> ### Anybody wrapped up in self is too small of a package to make a difference.

SECTION FIVE

CHAPTER SIXTEEN:
The Art of Giving

There truly is an art to giving, whether the contribution is in the form of effort, time, experience, influence, or cold hard cash. And nothing matches the soul-nourishing enlightenment of knowing that even a simple gift can make a difference in others' lives. No gift is insignificant—none too small or too large.

Let me use some metaphors, if you will. Our communities are our homes, play places, the curse of our luck, and the inspiration in our lives. They are our horizons, hopes, dreams, and visions for the future. But there's more. Around the corner, there's a corner community center. Sixty years of weathered memories and still standing against the elements. Strong, proud, indifferent to the wind and rain. But when you look closely, there's a bend in the structure and tilt to the east. That's a signal that we should start.

If we don't put our efforts into bridging capital to our communities, that community center around the corner will start to sag. We'll say, "Oh, we might want to do something." Still, before we know it, the timbers will rot; the roof will collapse; and the place that provided a gymnasium, library, kitchen, shelter, dances, work, security, and hope will come crashing down. We'll be left to remember the good and the bad, mostly the falling down.

On the other hand, if you're inclined to do something about your home, business, or community, there are hundreds of ways you can make a difference. I'm a champion of community organizations, so you've got the choice of whether you want to start one yourself or join in what will likely be a genuinely rewarding experience!

Community groups run from professional service agencies to neighborhood groups that form ideas into block parties and aim for the stars. You can hear about them in libraries, day salons, or barbershops. They include school groups, churches, unions, social-service groups, fraternities, clubs, and work organizations.

Their goals range from ensuring street safety and parking to rehabilitating neighborhoods, opening essential businesses, expanding learning centers, dedicating parks and playgrounds, preserving historic buildings, and providing affordable housing. There's more, and you've probably got ideas of your own. There's strength in numbers.

If you want to join a group or are already working toward finding funding solutions for your own business, look for the existing economic and community development organizations in your area. Participating in those groups can help revitalize your community while opening the doors to a collaboration with your own company and will expand your client base.

The collaboration will also help you stay updated on local causes and city and state policies that may affect your plans and business. Interpreting the economic and social landscape from new perspectives helps you stay proactive.

Local government agencies and organizations (schools, libraries, fire and police departments) that provide community services are also great places to expend effort in the form of time and support. Most undercapitalized communities are made up of dedicated, overworked citizens committed to their cause. Your support will be appreciated and can have an immediate and sure impact.

Businesses that cultivate a generous social conscience benefit from improved employee morale, and everyone enjoys being part of an inspiring story that makes a palpable difference in their community.

Those changes can be enhanced by establishing relationships with other organizations with your values and mission. Joining a cause with nonprofits with reasonable and authentic goals can help create a stronger culture and strengthen you and your employees. And if local events are on tap, they provide great places to reward your employees for their hard work by sponsoring them at sporting events, concerts, 5k community runs, Memorial Day picnics, or even bake sales, if that's what's on the calendar.

Events and sponsorships help the community and allow your business to interact and mingle with other businesses and their representatives. Change starts with you, so share your ideas, engage your friends and neighbors in conversation, and pool your knowledge. Everything is possible when we take the first step and work together. It's worth the fight!

Vision is setting the end first and then backing up and beginning.

CHAPTER SEVENTEEN:
Thought and Purpose in People

Investing in People through Leadership Initiatives

No matter how I have discussed and defined B*ridging Capital for Impact* and impact investing, it refers to investments that address social problems and potential issues and drive change. The investments cannot only be financial, however, as the transfer of wisdom and knowledge to the people within these communities is inherently meaningful.

Teach a man to fish so that he can catch his food, eat, feed others, and teach others to fish too. It is this process of paying it forward that matters. We can infuse capital into a community, and when we combine it with intellectual capital, nothing can stop us! There are examples of well-known celebrities who have done this very thing, and there are examples of individuals who are, for the most part, unknown and who have dedicated their lives to helping others. Pete Kadens, a Chicago millionaire who retired at forty, created a charity called Hope Chicago that will pay for the in-state college tuition, room and board, and books for thirty thousand Chicago high school students. In this deliberate act of giving, he has inspired the next generation to think bigger and beyond themselves.

The infusion of money without leadership is of minimal value when compared to the impact leadership and intervention can have on the existing and subsequent generations. So, like I have mentioned earlier, I had my moment of divine intervention at the bus stop, and I was determined to rise to the opportunity given to me.

We must be willing to pay it forward, both economically and intellectually, to invest in the underserved communities around us.

Leadership matters, and as impact investors seek to make investments that benefit society and impact communities, it is imperative to understand the importance of communication.

Capital is the lifeblood of our economy, of civilization. Without it, there is only chaos. And access to capital should be a fundamental right of every person. It improves lives, provides hope and understanding, and allows communities to thrive. Families use credit to buy homes, manage their affairs, educate their children, open businesses, and build communities.

Government spending and corporate philanthropy are beautiful things, but there is a growing need for increased investment opportunities targeting underserved communities and providing financial and social return stability. And those returns should be available for the borrowers and the lenders.

As individuals, we can invest our capital and time in making social improvements, and we should be able to do so without restraints. We must also be committed to investing in a transfer of knowledge about the things we know and have learned along the way in the same way that we endeavor to invest in our own families and ourselves.

Knowledge is Power – Only if it is put into action!

Poet and lyrical genius Sean Carter, aka Jay-Z, whose song "Legacy"— the upbeat track from the 4:44 album—discusses not only the legacy of the Carter family name but also the importance of legacy building within the community. That commitment is sometimes hard to tether, channel, focus, and direct. Wise people have added: The value of a man should be seen in what he gives and not in what he can receive.

I would add that as necessary capital is, we must all realize the obvious. It is not enough. It's never enough to just give someone money. Imagine the young lottery winner or professional athlete who suddenly comes into millions of dollars yet lacks the strength or wisdom to care for it. Imagine someone in an underserved community without access to capital, business advice, or mentorship about starting a small business.

I see our investment obligation to these communities as more than just capital. Like my mentor did, we must be willing to pause and take time to develop the programs and leadership courses, seminars, and events that can genuinely instill lasting change.

Defining the Private Sector

Each of us possesses a myriad experiences and gifts and a collection of life lessons we have received along the way. To pay it forward means to invest in others by transferring our knowledge, and that's where true legacy begins. It can be multiplied when we pour into others what we know. When we know better, we do better.

One of the life lessons I endeavor to teach my kids is to be confident. Confidence comes from the inside out, yet people and external forces can erode it—if you're not intentional about who you are.

Be confident in who you are, and don't let anyone take that away from you.

My son Jefferson is in high school, and my wife and I, as parents, began establishing the root of confidence when he was in kindergarten. But as we all know, other kids can be brutal.

Kids will tease you for what you don't have and what you do have. When I was growing up, I remember we would tease kids with a father figure for having what we didn't have. Jefferson was raised with a different mindset and more opportunities, but still, he used to be teased for his haircut. I'd take him for a haircut every two weeks, which was a luxury I certainly never had growing up.

But after the kids teased him about it, eventually, he didn't want to get his bi-weekly haircut.

Some of the lessons kids learn growing up come from the kids around them and not the adults. Some never have the opportunity to experience what it's like to have a mentor who cares enough to give them leadership and life lessons.

Pivotal points in life matter. We all have them, and they often lead to exponential growth. Is it possible to give a man a fish and teach him to fish at the same time? Through collective collaboration, we can.

Albert Einstein once said, *"If you find it in your heart to care for somebody else, you will have succeeded."*

Bridging capital is precisely about that. It is about investing in people and the communities they live in.

How can we serve others better?

How can we invest in the infrastructure and create leaders who care within those communities simultaneously?

When I think of leaders that came before me, there are many that come to mind.

Maya Angelou said, *"The difference between a dreamer and a visionary is that a dreamer has his eyes closed, and a visionary has his eyes open."*

Muhammad Ali said, *"Don't count the days. Make the days count."*

So often, we let life pass by as we struggle to get a good grip on things. Ali reminds us to take the reins into our own hands so that we make the most of every moment, rather than waiting for moments to fall into our laps.

If you feel that you won't succeed at any time, that's fine. Nobody knows for sure what will work and what won't, but we never know until we try. It's all right if we find a dozen ways to write a grant that doesn't work before finding one that does! We may also find six ways to set up a meeting with a councilperson that don't work or find only one way to fund our organization that does work. Effort equals purpose and success.

When things do go right, remember that you deserve the outcome. You can be gracious and self-conscious, but your drive and efforts produced the change you strove for and inspired. So, relish your accomplishments and refuse to believe anyone who doubts your sincerity and drive to make things happen.

Instead, enlist them to make a change with you!

Low-income communities deserve safe roads, good lighting, walking paths, and a positive atmosphere with thriving businesses and affordable housing. In addition, the people in these communities deserve access to community programs funded by the city or local entrepreneurs, such as business startup and personal leadership courses, policing, education, and good healthy options in grocery stores.

Revitalization helps revive these communities without forcing long-time inhabitants out of their homes. It's essential to understand the difference because blindly lashing out at people making improvements for the communities who need it most will deter others from trying to help in the future.

In Texas, we're experiencing both gentrification and revitalization, like many other states. Unfortunately, progress can be deceptive until years after projects are complete. Iconic neighborhoods are being reconstructed, and investors are adding expensive high-rise apartments, coffee shops, and chain stores or boutiques on well-lit streets. It may look nice from the outside, but the impact on the older existing residents cannot be ignored. Prices, taxes, and products have become unaffordable. Apartments are rented out on Air BNB or, as in the case of some small Colorado towns, are unavailable for local workers. In crested Butte, a once sleepy Colorado mountain town, investors bought so much property that the workers had nowhere to live. Massage therapists working in expensive hotels slept in their cars or tents at night for months. This is a product of gentrification when the community does not account for the cost of living for its workers.

In Texas, where growth has been explosive in recent years, some communities are unrecognizable. One neighborhood experiencing gentrification in Dallas-Fort Worth is Downtown Carrollton, a hip, newly built-up area.

There are empty fields where low-income apartments used to be, and the families living in them were forced to leave.

Small businesses were pushed out and replaced with expensive apartments and parking garages.

One example of successful revitalization, however, is not far from there; it is in South Dallas near Fair Park. The neighborhood is part of the Frazier Revitalization, an independent 501(c)(3) nonprofit organization established to create a mixed-income community that integrates current residents with new residents. Fifty percent of residents in the Frazier neighborhood are living under the poverty line. So instead of taking over the neighborhood, the Frazier Revitalization is working to provide resources to low-income residents and attempting to bring them out of poverty by opening new businesses.

To combat the aforementioned challenges, the Frazier Revitalization provides resources to help residents. For example, public transportation is accessible with a DART train running through the city, and a health center located at the train station provides affordable care for low-income residents.

There are several examples of communities that have thrived after the investment of financial and relational capital. It's incumbent upon each of us to drive change and monitor progress through our collective collaboration. Gentrification is a serious issue wherein typically rich, white people take over low-income areas predominantly inhabited by people of color. They raise the cost of living for that area and drive the original inhabitants out of the neighborhood. We should protect low-income communities of color from gentrification, but recently I've noticed how people have a tendency to claim gentrification every time construction starts in an old neighborhood.

This book was written with two central purposes in mind: (1) to educate and inform, and (2) to encourage and invoke execution. This further validates my commitment to reinvesting my time, talents, and treasures into the community that helped position me for greatness. Therefore, I have written this book to share my knowledge and insight and encourage like-minded individuals to embrace the book as a resource and tool for impact investing in in the hope that they take concrete action toward these objectives.

The people who reside in undercapitalized communities are not just numbers. They are the inspiration and the genesis for bridging capital with measurable impacts. Today, some people will call it ESG Investing, Sustainable Financing, and/or Social Impact Investing.

When we look into the eyes of our fellow human beings and see despair, this should provide us with ample motivation to bridge capital into undercapitalized communities. We all strive to live and prosper, hoping our descendants and community will advance to the next level and leave a meaningful history for future generations.

Bridging Capital for Impact is the deliberate, organized, and conscious effort by members of society to construct balanced communities through collective collaboration!

**You cannot separate a
leaders words & his walk in life.**

CHAPTER EIGHTEEN:

Jeffrey D. Powell | The Silent American Asset™

Personal Experience

In my youth, I was always fascinated with numbers, and I enjoyed having conversations about them with individuals who were older than me. They would often tell me, "Son, you have an old soul; your talk tells me you have been here before." As a child, I never knew what that expression meant. Fast forward to the present day, and I very well appreciate the ten thousand-plus hours that have been invested into my interests by my aunts, uncles, grandparents, mother, and family friends.

I was reared in a single-parent household by a young, strong, independent woman who let her actions speak much louder than her words. But unfortunately, my mother's high school education was disrupted in the '70s with the unplanned birth of her first and only son, Jeffrey D. Powell.

My mother left high school to provide for the two of us and invested her extra time into my development. Even though she never finished high school, education was incredibly important to my mother, and she ensured I never missed a day of school. In fact, I had perfect attendance for thirteen years straight—if you include pre-k—and I have the certificate to prove it.

When I graduated from high school, I recall my mother kissing me on my forehead, holding both of my ears, and looking me in my eyes. She said, "Son, you make me proud, but you are just getting started." And she was right; high school was only the beginning; it was to be followed by college, the walk of life, and my Wall Street profession.

Professional Experience

Jeffrey D. Powell is an independent thinker, author, and one of the most notable experts on the topic of bridging capital for community impact.

Jeff serves as the senior vice president of the Wells Fargo & Co. Government & Institutional Banking Group. He focuses on delivering financial solutions to large municipalities and educational institutions, utilizing the bank's robust menu of capabilities. His direct responsibilities include analyzing and securing both on-balance and off-balance sheet credit lending strategies in Texas and Louisiana.

Prior to joining Wells Fargo Bank, N.A., Jeff's past executive experience included being the vice president of sales and investment banking at Merrill Lynch and vice president at JP Morgan Chase in the Private Wealth Management Group, where he managed equity and debt portfolios for both public and private clients.

Jeff received his undergraduate degree from The College at Brockport in Upstate New York. He completed the Harvard Kennedy School Public Policy Leadership Credential in 2021 and is prepared to bridge the credential into a Master in Public Policy. He holds multiple NASD securities licenses in addition to his Corporate Financial Planning and Analysis Certification from the College for Financial Planning.

Jeff is an active board member and community humanitarian in both New York and Texas. His former and present advisory board positions include the Houston Habitat for Humanity, Houston Homeless SEARCH, co-chairmanship of the Buffalo Soldiers National Museum Building Fund Raising, membership of the Texas Southern University School of Business Fellowship Board, and co-chairmanship of the Wheeler Avenue Baptist Church Finance Committee. He is also a member of the United Way of Greater Houston Project Blueprint Class XXIV, Leadership Houston Class XXXII, and American Leadership Forum Class XLII.

Jeff was recognized as one of Houston Business Journal's "40 under 40" Future Leaders in 2013.

Passion and Purpose

I can still recall the words of my late grandmother: *"Skills cost one dollar, but passion is priceless."* She firmly believed that my passion for numbers and my willingness to help people discern the value of the dollar was a gift from above.

Her words of encouragement encouraged my passion for fulfilling my purpose, and in the end, it became my profession. My fascination with numbers and structuring capital solutions helped propel my professional career and what I call my personal passion projects.

Finding your passion is not just about finding a career or making money. It is about finding your authentic self and applying your

God-given talents in a way that will impact lives today and in the future.

I never knew numbers could mean so much,
and so little at the same time – J. Powell

jeffreydpowell.com